Oct 202

To Mam

From Richard & Sharon

The Clyde

INVERARY
St Catherines
Glencroe
Tarbet
Strachur
Ben Lomond
Furnace
Lachlan Castle
Minard Castle
Loch Gilphead
Ardrishaig
Loch Eck
Loch Long
Loch Lomond
Luss
Gareloch Head
Shandon
Ardentinny
Blairmore
Kilmun
Sandbank
Roseneath
Helensburgh
Alexandria
Balloch
Bonhill
Dunoon
Kirn
Gourock
GREENOCK
Dumbarton
Kilpatrick Hills
Old Kilpatrick
Bowling
Dalmuir
Yoker
Renfrew
Govan
Paisley
Inverkip
Skelmorlie
Knock Cas.
Largs
Kelburn Cas.
Fairlie
Millport
Great Cumbrae
Little Cumbrae
Inellan
Toward Pt
Wemyss Bay
Rothesay
Ascog
Kames
Tighnabruaich
Ormidale House
Glendaruel
Loch Riddon
Loch Striven
Bute
Ettrick Bay
Ardlamont Point
Inch Marnoch
Loch Fyne
Knapdale
Tarbert
Skipness
Kintyre
Carradale Castle
Carradale Bay
Saddell Castle
Saddell Bay
Campbeltown
Davarr I.
Southend
Sanda Sound
Sanda
L. Ranza
The Cock of Arran
Catacol
Carroch Head
Thundergay
Whitefarland
Dougrie
Caint-na-Galliach
Goat Fell
Ben Noosh
Corrie
Brodick Castle
Brodick
Auchingallan
Druidical Circle
Machry Bay
Glen Cloy
Shisken
Lamlash
Holy I.
Whiting Bay
Blackwater Foot
Sliddery
Kildonan Pt
Pladda I.
Portencross
West Kilbride
Ardrossan
Saltcoats
Irvine
Irvine Bay
Troon
Lady Isle
Prestwick
Ayr Bay
AYR
Heads of Ayr
Maybole
Culzean Castle
Turnberry Castle & Point
Kirkoswold
Ailsa Craig
Girvan
Ballantrae
Scale
1 2 3

A
Sketch Map
of the
CLYDE
River Forth
Campsie Fells
Kilsyth Hills
EDINBURGH
Yoker
Scotstown
Partick
Govan
GLASGOW
Airdrie
Coatbridge
R. Calder
Uddingston
Holytown
Rutherglen
Pollokshaws
Cambuslang
Bellshill
Mothetwell
High Blantyre
Hamilton
Dalziel
Wishaw
Chatelherault
Cadzow Castle
Cambusnethan Ho.
Larkhall
Dalserf
Mauldslie
Carluke
Milburn
Rosebank
Nethanfoot
Crossford
Craignethan Castle
Stonebyres Linn
LANARK
Carstairs
Carnwath
Kirkfieldbank
New Lanark
Corra Linn
Hyndford Br.
Bonnington
Nethan Water
Covington
Biggar
PEEBLES
Thankerton
Symington
Tinto Hill
Culter
Lamington Tower
Lamington
Roberton
R. Tweed
Wallaces Cas.
Abington
Tweedsmuir
Crawford
Elvanfoot Sta.
Clydes Law
Source of Clyde
Camp
Leadhills
Lowther Hills
Clydes Burn
Roman Rd.
Daer W.
Beattock
English Miles
1 2 3 4 5 6 7 8 9 10
20
E. M. Carter

The Clyde

RIVER AND FIRTH

described by

Neil Munro

with illustrations by
Mary Y. and J. Young Hunter

The Grimsay Press

The Grimsay Press
An imprint of Zeticula
57, St Vincent Crescent
Glasgow
G3 8NQ
Scotland
http://www.kennedyandboyd.co.uk

First published in 1907 by Adam and Charles Black as *The Clyde; River and Firth painted by Mary Y. and J. Young Hunter described by Neil Munro.*

First published in this form in 2010

ISBN 978-1-84530-084-5

The Official Website of the Neil Munro Society
is at http://www.neilmunro.co.uk/

Contents

Contents

Contents

List of Illustrations

List of Illustrations

List of Illustrations

CHAPTER I

INTRODUCTORY

As, in ordinary life, great material success, and the romantic, artistic, and loveable qualities are seldom found in the same person, so in States, cities, and rivers we give our custom as traders to the powerful and prosperous, but our affections to the humble, the fallen, the futile. Chicago or Birmingham for our invested capital; Venice and Bruges for our honeymoons and our dreams! The name of the Mersey or the Tyne may stir the hearts of Lloyds and the coal trade, but the Avon and the Severn have charms for the imagination which are in despite of Bristol or Cardiff; and the Dove and Derwent, though we may never have seen them, minister to our sentiments far more than does the Humber, to whose commercial greatness they contribute the mossy waters of the Pennine wells, leaving their poetry behind them, like wise business men, before they come to the malted Trent or the silk-mills of Derby. If the Thames can still be great in commerce, and beloved in literature and art, it is because she is not one river, but many. Her upper waters still retain the glamour of the Prothalamion, though she becomes a drab at London, and in her lower reaches can only stir the heart of a poetic sailor like Joseph Conrad.

It is so in Scotland, too; the Tweed—the obscure, unprofitable Tweed—gets all the glory of allusion in story, poem, and song, awakening by her very name, in quiet and distant chambers, thoughts of Merlin and haunted hall, castles, harps, men-at-arms, and a thousand phantoms out of books; while the Clyde, her far more richly gifted sister naturally, has merely the fame of trade. To the world which knows her not, but only as a name on maps, shipping lists, and bills of lading, the Clyde, I fear, will ever be a drudge of commerce, a scullery-maid of Glasgow, yet we who know her truly must sigh to have her so misunderstood, and grudge a little the purely adventitious honours of the Tweed, whose fame is not a consequence of her natural features, but of human association and the hypnotic influence of genius.

Once upon a time, when Abbotsford was still a *château en Espagne*, Walter Scott had offered to him as a residence part of the castle of Craignethan, near the Clyde, a time-ennobled edifice, which has the longer lease in men's affections since he gave it the name of Tillietudlem. Not even the gifts that James Watt and Henry Bell bequeathed for the future greatness of the Clyde can wholly reconcile us to the loss our river sustained by the Wizard's hesitating refusal of the opportunity. Had he come here—who knows?—

the vale of Clyde to-day might have been redolent of romance, familiar and endeared to all lovers of English letters, for men and women are apt to see no beauty anywhere until authority directs them, and there was plenty of material on the banks of Clyde to rouse the fire and speed the pen of Scott. But his imagination fed, as the imagination of genius always will, on scenes that held the memory of irrecoverable youth; the Borders had no rival in his love; Ettrick and Yarrow, Melrose, Dryburgh, Abbotsford, and Gala are therefore Tweedside names that stir the mind of culture like trumpet-calls, and the Clyde is—— Glasgow!

So at least the world thinks. For such as have eyes and their own imaginations, independent of the guidance of poet or novelist, the Clyde is, none the less, the most astonishing, beautiful, and inspiring of Scottish waterways. Not wholly to protect the lush green straths from the guerilla and hill-cumbered north did Lollius Urbicus build the Roman wall from Clyde to Forth. If there were fertile fields, the richest in Albyn, worth the Empire's strict defending, there were also, we may be sure, in the valley of the Clyde, a people with steadfast homes—the kind of people Rome preferred to conquer—and round even the first settled homes are always found association, legend, song, and history, and the things that tempt to peacefulness and order. These the vallum sheltered and encouraged, "bridling the wild Highlandman" more effectively than ever did the Forth. Even now, within the sight of railways or the sound of shipyard sirens, there is something awe-inspiring in the relics of that long green ridge across the country, marking the line of vigil and defence—desolate, silent, producing peaceful crops or giving habitation to the weasel and the lark. Where the sentinel paced between the forts, the ear of fancy may restore the clink of bronze accoutrements, the challenge of the night, across the ditch the hoarse defiance of the Picts. It was so long ago—and yet, for all the land has changed in salient features, it might have been but yesterday! The hill-sides still record that alien occupation in sites of camp and fort, and trails that mark the roadway of the legionaries—vague monuments of the old appreciation, commercial rather than poetic. Rome's troops withdrawn, and the vallum, once so strong, a crumbling heap of turves for birds to build in, the Clyde became the backbone of a kingdom long before red Flodden gave to Tweed a melancholy charm. St. Kentigern and Christianity; Wallace and the War of Independence; the struggle of Kirk and State—the story of these men and these movements is inextricably interwoven with Strathclyde.

The Clyde also, like the Thames, when one comes to think of it, is not one river, but three, so wholly different are her character and destiny at different parts. For miles below her mountain origin she presents an aspect primitive, beautiful, and desirable, as she must have seemed seventeen hundred years ago even to homesick alien conquerors, and the moors, farms, and orchards are unchanged from what they must have been when the Covenanters sheltered in the deep ravines. Then, at Blantyre, commerce claims her, and makes of her a different river—the river the world knows best, that builds and bears the argosies of all the nations, and makes a sullen and degraded way through a great city, to change yet again into a different creature in her estuary that woos the cleansing hills. It is the estuary that to-day peculiarly redeems the name of Clyde from sordid association, and the Firth of Clyde is unequalled by any other approach into Europe. " It is Europe, abridged and assorted, and passed before you in the space of a few hours," says John Burroughs the American, " the highlands and lochs and castle-crowned crags on the one hand, and the lowlands, with their parks and farms, their manor halls and matchless verdure on the other."

To get the best impressions of the Clyde, then, one should come to her as Burroughs came, without prejudice, straight out of the western ocean, to wake some sunny morning in a channel clasped by far-extending promontories, broken by mountainous isles; and sail into the upper basin, where the ship will seem to float in an inland lake encompassed by hills; to pass again on the crest of the tide beyond Greenock into the actual river, that leads by verdant meadows and waving fields of corn so close at hand that from the cabin may be heard the landrail's call, into the city twenty miles away, where new ships spring to life with furious din of hammers, and old ones lie tethered for miles along the quays, longing for the sea and the distant port again. And having left his ocean liner, one should follow otherwise the course of Clyde, that for other fifty miles runs deviously through a valley that is the abstract, the epitome of all the Scottish Lowlands. That is the best way to see the Clyde, but it is the more uncommon, since the modern traveller comes by road, as did the Romans, and so, too, often returns without having any idea that the pride of the modern Clyde is in her estuary.

What modern Scotland might have been without the Clyde it is curious to contemplate, for on the river and on its neighbourhood depends the greater part of her prosperity. It might almost seem to have been by the merest fluke of nature that the West of Scotland owns the river now. A glance at the map reveals that near Biggar its course approaches within seven miles of the Tweed. The watershed lies between, but so little above the level of the Clyde that a trivial excavation would divert the latter into Tweeddale. "That it once took that course," says Professor Geikie, "thus entering the sea at Berwick instead of at Dumbarton, is probable, and if some of the gravel mounds at Thankerton could be re-united it would do so again." Yet the Clyde could doubtless well enough afford to part with its present head waters, since its greatest feeders join it west of the watershed further down, and by another name its influence on Scotland would have been no less. There would still have been "Cornes, Meeds, Pastorage, Woods, Parks, Orchards, Castles, Pallaces, divers kinds of Coale and earth-fewell" in the valley, which, with a patriot's ecstasy, the traveller William Lithgow called the "Paradice of Scotland." But Clydesdale's treasure-house was not an orchard bower; it lay in the veins of coal and ironstone underneath, and was buried in the mud that silted up the narrow channel into which the wide, wild swamp of the early ages had long attenuated. Wanting either the carboniferous measures of old Strathclyde, or a natural highway to the western sea, the Scottish midlands would have had a different destiny. Together they combined to make the greatness of twentieth century Glasgow; and Glasgow, whether we like it or not, is the heart of modern Scotland.

It is Glasgow's boast that she made the Clyde; and, indeed, the claim is not, in a sense, unjustified, since the Clyde was merely beautiful before she took it in hand, and turned twenty miles of hazardous and shallow stream, where a coracle could venture but with peril, into a channel fit to bear with safety the greatest vessels of our time. In its proper place I shall treat of this presumptuous and gallant enterprise, which won for the Clyde renown among the merchants, a name for commerce that has cost her the loss of a different and more perfumed reputation for charms of which she has only in part been ravished.

CHAPTER II

THE SOURCE

Looking on our river at any part near its deliverance to the cleansing sea; looking on it from the wharves, where it seems to clot among the piles, and fouls anew the sides of its native ships that have been washed and purified by voyages of a thousand miles; or from the docks in which, part-prisoned, it sulks and smells; or, indeed, seeing it anywhere from Blantyre to Bowling, more or less a degraded drab, spoiled by man for his profit and pleasure, and yet making him pay for it somehow and smartly, one must often think of its clean and innocent origin, far up in the Lanarkshire hills. Not even there, of course, is its real origin. It is in the heavens, in the flying cisterns of cloud, or in the sea itself, to which it is ever returning—the sea that every drop in every river in the world remembers as its home. But the conception of the circle of all things, the sense of the eternity of matter, the certainty that nothing had an origin and nothing shall have an end, is too big for us to grasp except in rapturous moments, and we arbitrarily fix upon the source of

THE SOURCE OF THE CLYDE

our river—really only an attenuate arm of the sea, an inseparable part of the same mighty water that pierces to the Andes as the Amazon, or elsewhere bears the purely local name of the Mackenzie—we establish it in a peat-brown rut somewhere among heather and the cry of whaup and plover.

It is not difficult to find this reputed source of the river that like a great artery swells to an ugly and unwholesome aneurism among Glasgow streets. I have scooped it all up in my hands, from a mossy cup in a nook of barren hill 1,550 feet above the level of the sea, in Crawford parish, near to Elvanfoot. Clean well water, a tiny eye of blue reflecting the sky above it; silent, seemingly motionless; content to be this and nothing else, an infant still unconscious of the future, thinking nothing of the rapids and the crashing falls, of the towns to be swept through, the fleets to be carried, its destiny of squalor and fame. I know its origin is disputed; I know that though Little Clydes Burn is the commonly-reputed head stream of the Clyde, and the rhyme says

"Annan, Tweed and Clyde,
Rise a' out o' ae hill-side,"

there is much to be said for the claims of the Daer Water, that flows from farther still, the slopes of Gadd Hill, within a quarter of a mile of the shire of Dumfries. But as in truth the decision must at best be arbitrary, I take the common one, and stick by the rivulet that rises in Clyde Law. For that I have many reasons—the best, that it is nearest Glasgow and most accessible. Furthermore, it is a pleasant place to go to, if, as when last I went, the weather favour by the right proportion of sun and cloud; to go to leisurely, not by the most obvious and easy route, which would be to take the train to Elvanfoot, but by more gradual ways, so that you see the river in its youth as well as in its cradle.

Old travellers from the south by stage-coach, having risen to Beattock Summit, 1,000 feet in air, with a flourish of the bugle horn, soon found themselves in the exhilarating society of the quickly growing Clyde. The road which still remains for the cyclist and the automobilist, who have reason to bless the well-bottomed, honest work of Telford, dead more than seventy years, keeps company with the river nearly all the way to Symington, and from Carlisle to Glasgow is a palimpsest on that more ancient highway along which the Romans marched from Hadrian's Wall, on the Solway, to the Wall of Antoninus, between the Clyde and Forth. We joined this road, going south, near Lamington, that to some of us was a discovery almost as important as the source of the Clyde. Bowered in beach and ash, its highways bordered by the trimmest of hedges, its village Arcadian, clean, and rural, gardened before the doors, dozing in the scent of flowers and the shadow of trees, it is destitute wholly of the squalid national features of many Scots hamlets, or of the no more loveable new features of some others that ape English architecture, or kill

LITTLE CLYDE FARM, SOURCE OF THE CLYDE

rusticity and erupt in villas to make a Glasgow holiday. The mile or so that separates Lamington from its railway station, and the conservatism of Lord Lamington (a thing I love in lairds when it does not inconvenience me), will long, I am sure, keep this sylvan district unspotted by the world. "Five furlongs off," as the guide-book says, in the quaint, old-fashioned, uninforming way of guide-books, is Lamington Tower, where, if you like to believe it (and it hurts you none to do so), Marion Bradfute, wife of William Wallace, was born. We saw its north-west wall in the distance, "child of loud-throated war," with the rooks cawing over the crumbling masonry; but, seeking more peaceful edifices, we went to St. Ninian's Church, where only a Norman arch remains to indicate the antiquity of ecclesiastical Lamington, and where once, on a cold and stormy day, Robert Burns sat among the worshippers, and heard a sermon which called forth a stinging epigram.

We drove by the river-side through Abington and Crawford, of which the most that can be said is that they thrive, and have a tonic air that city doctors more and more prescribe to their patients. We left behind tall Tinto, whose suave contour minimises the impression of its height. Scores, and possibly hundreds, of anglers waded in the river, casting assiduously, and, let us hope, with more sport than was apparent. Over all—the billowy hills, green, gold, and brown; the sheltered holms, the farms, the towers, the linking river; the sky spread out enormously, with fleecy silver clouds, or menacing black ones, chasing across its vivid blue. More bare than further down in the dale of orchards under Lanark, the valley still had its peculiar and arresting charm. On such days must the Roman legionaries have often stepped aside from the great North Road, or wandered from the camps near Elvanfoot, and looked along its alien landscape, sorrowful a little, missing rust-red roofs and the flush of vines, but feeling the happy pang that comes from vistas spacious and swept by sun.

I cannot deny that we were tempted in such weather to seek an origin for our river more remote than little Clydes Burn, for the day was long, and the opposite side of the valley, where rise the romantic Lowthers, had a rare alluring aspect. There, really, say others, runs the Clyde, though with another name, and with a silver spoon in its mouth in the shape of silver seams that long ago made fortunes for the men who worked them. Dalveen Pass, Enterkin Pass, and the Mennock—their sombre recesses have sheltered the hunted sons of the Covenant, and inspired the passionate prose of Defoe and Dr. John Brown. The Enterkin, and Wanlockhead, and the Leadhills have their Laureate; it is significant of how far a wandering race we are, and how fond our memories of home, that I found him recently an exile in Montreal. In Robert Reid's "Ballad of Kirkbride" is to be found what is perhaps the best Covenanting poem ever written, and its atmosphere is that of the austere yet beautiful Lowther hills where he was born:—

TINTO, AND THE CLYDE VALLEY AT ABINGTON

The Source

"Bury me in Kirkbride
Where the Lord's redeemed anes lie!
The auld kirkyard on the grey hill-side
Under the open sky;
Under the open sky.
Or the breist o' the braes sae steep,
And side by side wi' the banes that lie
Streiked there in their hinmaist sleep.
This puir dune body maun sune be dust;
But it thrills wi' a stound o' pride,
To ken it may mix wi' the great and just
That slumber in thee, Kirkbride!

"Wheest! did the saft win' speak?
Or a yaumerin' nicht-bird cry?
Did I dream that a warm haun' toucht my cheek,
And a winsome face gaed by?
And a winsome face gaed by.
Wi' a far-aff licht in its een—
A licht that bude come frae the dazzlin' sky,
For it spak o' the starnies' sheen.
Age may be donart, and dazed and blin',
But Ise warrant, whate'er betide,
A true heart there made tryst wi' my ain,
And the tryst-word seemed—'Kirkbride.'"

But we resisted the temptations to those farther head-waters, and, from the farm called Little Clyde, near Elvanfoot, walked up the hill for little more than a mile to what is most popularly accepted as our river's source. It was an easy walk, beside a burn that tumbled not too hurriedly from the hill; a burn at first with musical little falls and brown pools, then quickly narrowing to little more than a deep drain, that tinkled so soft it did not even drown the hum of bees; then suddenly losing itself entirely in a fold of the hill, to find the sun again a few yards further on in the tiny spring that is the veritable source of Clyde. A hat could cover it. We sat beside it, and ate for appetite, and drank to the glory and honour of all rivers, but specially to Clyde, the mother of our fortunes.

Said one, inspired and mischievous, with the cork of a hock-bottle in his hand, "Let us cork the source, and fly, and see what happens," and foolishly we did so, then hurried like criminals down the hillside to the valley. We caught the Glasgow train at Elvanfoot, and sat among unsuspicious fellow-passengers, who did not know that day a dire deed had been done. We did not dare to look out, but guiltily sat behind our papers, thinking of the dreadful consequences of our folly—of the anglers suddenly finding themselves in the muddy bed of an arrested river; of the first stillness of innumerable centuries coming upon Corra Linn and Bonnington, where erst the cataract roared; of Bothwell's ruin aghast over an empty, arid chasm; of Glasgow horrified to find her ships heeled over in the fetid ooze, her proud commercial eminence destroyed mysteriously in an hour; of a tide that lapped in from the estuary upon wide and slimy banks at Erskine Ferry, waiting for ships that would come down no more, but must rot on their sides by wharves made desolate by the cork of a bottle of hock. A vital blow, in faith! from Germany.

WHERE THE DUNEATON WATER JOINS
THE CLYDE (NEAR ABINGTON)

The Source

But when we came into the city, and looked from the railway bridge in the dusk of the falling night, we saw the river quite unchanged. The harbour lights shone on the same wide, oily waste of water that we loathe and reverence. A thousand spars struck black against the last faint glow of the west; hulls swung to their hawsers; tug-boats puffed and darted by either bank. One ship, huge and mighty, in mid-channel, slid seaward to the night, to some unknown adventure.

CHAPTER III

FROM THE TOP OF TINTO

To see the career of the upper Clyde in one comprehensive glance while aeroplanes are still impracticable and balloons are scarce, demands the escalade of Tinto. It is no serious Alpine business climbing from Symington to the great cairn that marks the summit of the hill 2300 feet above sea level, 1700 above the river; the apparent ease of the ascent is even tempting, and the view from the top would be sufficient reward for greater exertions than are really involved. Tinto is lord of Clydesdale—"hill of fire" they say it means, alluding to its ancient Druid altars. It dominates the mind, tradition and history of the country as markedly as it does the moors and glens and lesser hills around it. Loftiest of the "southern heights of the central Lowlands"; standing on the common border of four parishes, with a dome that from far sheep-folds in other counties, and from the streets of distant manufacturing towns, commands the eye by blunt bulk rather than by majesty, myth wraps it, as vague and tenuous as the mists that so often drag around its shoulders; and

ROBERTON

each Scottish traveller coming north by rail, and seeing it on his left as he swoops from the heights of Beattock, murmurs cryptic words that state

> "On Tintock tap there is a mist
> And in that mist there is a kist";

or perhaps, in more cynical mood,

> "But tho' a lass were ere so black,
> Let her hae a penny siller,
> Set her up on Tinto tap,
> The wind will blaw a man till her."

Parts of sixteen counties are to be seen from the summit—from the Grampians and Goatfell to the Bass, from Cumberland to Ireland—but, what is more to our purpose, we can follow the windings of the Clyde almost from its origin till it crashes over Corra Linn near Lanark. It trots from Elvanfoot among the lesser hills—the tail-end of the "Laws" of the Lowthers, "Gills," "Riggs," and "Dods," that speak of a different occupation in the past from that which gave Gaelic appellations to the mountains of the Firth. Soon it babbles innocently to the ear of old Tower Lindsay or Castle Crawford, held as the Barony's heart in the reign of William the Lion in lordship of "Sweyne the Son of Thor," a fact which shows how far the Viking conquest pierced beyond the coast. Tower Lindsay's moat is dry; its walls have been ruins for generations; Wallace is said to have attacked and destroyed it when it was full of English soldiers; later it was the home of Archibald Bell-the-Cat. And yet a little further down the stream which washes its rocky promontory on three sides are the scanty relics of another fortalice, whose pastoral cognomen, the Bower of Wandell, holds for us poetic thoughts that may have been wholly absent from its first designators. On a site that danger only would dictate, the Bower of Wandell may have aged and perished without a single hour of war, its sole surviving tradition being that for a while it was a hunting-seat for James V., and the cell for a kingly quarry, Marjory Weir, "The Flower of Nethan."

Here the strath opens out fertile and wooded, with wide fields, fragrant of immemorial harvests. As early as the twelfth century three brothers settled in it, round the base of Tinto; their names were Robert, Wice or Wicens, and Lambin, and their respective homesteads are marked now by the villages of Roberton, Wiston, and Lamington. They were pleasantly situated in the shadow of Tinto, that helped to shelter them from northern storms. It is here, indeed, the Clyde itself hesitates among the haughs, as if inclined to resume the old Tweedward way, and it is only by a sudden doubling back at Culter that it remains true to us. As we see from Tinto, it is not far from Culter to Biggar, which is on a totally different water-shed, and does not figure on the bathy-orographical map of the Clyde at all. Yet Biggar counts itself in Clydesdale. A town with a witty perception of its own importance ("London's big, but Biggar's Biggar"), it

THE RIVER AT LAMINGTON

has grown up through centuries under the aegis of the Lords Fleming, who are supposed to have settled here in the reign of David I. Over their castle—Boghall, half a mile south of the town—the moss and the nettle triumph now, though once it was among the noblest edifices in the South of Scotland. The Flemings fought with Bruce; it was one of them who held aloft the bleeding head of Comyn after Bruce had slain him, and said, "Let the dead shaw," which became the family's motto. Edward II. lodged some nights in Boghall; in 1565 it sheltered briefly Mary Queen of Scots, whose guardians had found therein one of the renowned "four Marys" who were her companions and playfellows in France—Mary Fleming, latterly wife of the notorious Maitland of Lethington.

But Biggar has more modern claims to historical importance; it holds the unmarked graves of William Ewart Gladstone's ancestors, who were farmers there for many generations. One of them was James Gledstone, a "stickit minister," who became rector of Leith Grammar School. Before he realised that destiny was against his preaching, he was very anxious that his brother John, who was a farmer, like his father before him, should hear him preach, and give a candid opinion on his qualifications. He held forth one day, accordingly, in Biggar Church, but threw away all hope of winning his brother's good opinion by reading his discourse. Coming down, he asked, "Now, John, what do you think of my performance to-day?" "Weel, Jamie," was the candid answer, "to tell the truth, I would as soon hear ane o' my ain nowt routing in the loan as hear you in the poopit."

From Covington, (a quaint old village where there is a pre-Reformation church,) to Hyndford Bridge we see the river sweep in a wide semi-circle, which in itself is so twined and twisted that a distance of twenty miles is run between points which in a straight line are not more than seven and a half miles apart. At the furthest point of the arc towards the north-east lies the old-fashioned village of Carnwath, a mile and a quarter from the river bank. For centuries the Somervilles—Norman barons, who came over with the Conqueror—held Carnwath lands; their tombs are in the ruins of the old Gothic church at the western end of the town; their castle of Couthally is a hardly distinguishable mark on the moor it used to dominate. In 1589 the Master of Somerville accidentally shot his younger brother, and, dying himself three years later, "the head was as clean taken off the house of Couthally as you would strike off the head of a sybba," in the phrase of a lugubrious but prescient commentator of the time, for the fortunes of the family declined from that hour, and the Somervilles were but a memory when Peden the prophet was preaching to the multitudes on the moor where their steeds had cantered.

Between Carnwath and Hyndford the river is the scene of two of the best ballads it has inspired—"Willie and Mary Margaret," the story of a lover drowned, and "Young Hyndford," with a similar tragic foundation. Carstairs, a small village half a

BONNINGTON FALLS

mile south-east of the Mouse Water, occupies the site of an old Caledonian and Roman town, Corin-caer, or Coria, and was apparently a place of some importance from the number and character of architectural and other Roman remains which have been frequently found in its neighbourhood. A more modern village has clustered round the Caledonian Railway Junction of Carstairs, where the main trunk railway diverges to Glasgow and Edinburgh.

Yet further to the west, though we lose the shining of the river, we see the woods of the glens in the orchard country—the Cartland, the Nethan, and the Garrion, deep and narrow gorges, where the broken men of the Covenant hid from the troopers of Claverhouse; and over them the great moors, from Douglas to the Mearns, broken by peat moss and hag, friendly to the footman, inimical to horse, and so the scene of the conventicles. Drumclog is there on the boggy side of Loudon Hill, where the first skirmish of the insurrection of 1679 was lost by Claverhouse—an insurrection not unwelcome, possibly inspired by the Government, which was for a speedy issue and an end to these troublesome people, who prayed with their hands on their weapons, a "gust of the spirit" in their bosoms, and their bonnets not too far scrugged down on their brows, lest they should miss the first sight of the enemy. To these glens and to these moors the towns we see to-day from Tinto contributed their refugees; the narrow Nethan glen itself harboured innumerable families from Lesmahagow, so it had such wild associations of alarum and death that it is no wonder phantom armies—as we are told by Patrick Walker—rose like an exhalation from the junction of its waters with the Clyde, and, having awed ecstatic witnesses, sank again to evening vapours by Crossford.

Below Crossford, where the valley widens into wider fields again, Carluke is within two miles and a half of the east bank of the river. It was anciently Forest Kirk. On elevated ground, the town, constituted a burgh of barony in 1662, commands an extensive and lovely view of the central portion of Strathclyde. It was in Forest Kirk that nobles of the country solemnly appointed William Wallace Guardian of Scotland; so at least claims local history, though elsewhere the distinction is credited to Selkirk in Ettrick Forest. Below it lies Milton Lockhart. In March, 1782, the river rose seventeen feet, flooding the holms that lie on the peninsula. A farmer in the neighbourhood—Greenshields—came into his kitchen, where the furniture was floating, and drew his arm-chair through the water to his usual place beside the fire. "Wife," said he, "put on the big kail-pat, and mak's some sweet-milk parritch, for I doot it'll be the last food we'll hae on earth."

These are the more obvious features of the valley which reveals itself below us as we stand on Tinto in the whistling south-west wind that sends us to the shelter of the cairn, but the fancy summons up scenes byegone that have left no sign on hill or moor. We look on the shattered tower and the tombs of men

THE BRINK OF CORRA LINN

departed, stones stained with blood and blackened with the fires of war, and mossy or weed-grown plots that once were garden pleasances, where men and women walked and loved and quarrelled, and live no more but as sounding names in history-books. We see douce, prosperous towns, industrious villages, mansions of living and lucky men, and it may seem for a moment that Strathclyde has changed. But when we look and think again, the change has been but trivial; though the crops be different, they are the same old fields. In her masses, in her larger features, nature never alters; Tinto stands as when the Beltane fires first scorched her lichens; the contours of the hills around her are as they were a thousand years ago; the river keeps its ancient course; the shadow of the mountain falls across the plain, shifting with the season as it did when the Roman felt the chill of it as he stood on sentry. There is still the old heather and the scent of unchanging flowers; the cuckoo chimes, and the black-cock calls in a language that would seem familiar as his mother tongue to any ancient Pict, if to-day, in ghostly semblance, he could come from his forgotten barrow in the bosom of the hills and listen to the voice of the afternoon.

CHAPTER IV

LANARK AND THE FALLS

A SYMPATHETIC passion for the wild and picturesque in nature is so modern, that the mountains of the Firth, which doubtless were no more than unpleasant and inconvenient mounds of earth to Agricola, and abominable protuberances to early eighteenth century travellers from the suave and sylvan south, must have kept the secret of their beauty and charm solely for the native eye. Even to the savage Caledonian without any theories of beauty—possibly, like the Hindu, ignorant of such a fine abstraction—there would be something dear in each familiar peak, each pass traversed on the hunt or foray, remembered in tranquillity. Captain Burt, who boasted in one of his "Letters from the North" that he never made one retrograde step when he was leaving the mountains, yet found it "pretty strange, though very true (by what charm I know not)," that he should have been "well enough pleased to see them again on my return from England, and this has made my wonder cease that a native should be so fond of such a country." Ossian Macpherson, Rousseau, the Romantic movement and

CORRA LINN

the increase of travel, revealed the beauty of the wild hills, made it so obvious to every modern eye, that we can hardly believe there was a time when they were regarded but as rude excrescences which marred true beauty, an attribute that for early thought was either smoothness, harmony, usefulness, goodness, or proportion alone. As with mountains so with water-falls. To Father Hennepin, the first white man who saw Niagara, the sight was hideous, the roar infernal, and yet to-day, with a fuller vision, we often ponder with regret on undiscovered cataracts in untracked wilds, glistening in the sun with no eye to see them, wasting their fragrance on the desert air.

Water-falls, however, had all the fascination of the new-discovered even so late as a hundred years ago, and travellers in the North invariably made a point of seeing those that ornament the Clyde. Gray, of the "Elegy," visited them in 1764, and thought the "landscape of woods and rocks worthy of the hand of a Poussin." When Wordsworth and his sister Dorothy, with Coleridge, drove from Leadhills circuitously by Crawfordjohn and Douglasdale (not by Elvanfoot, as the latest editor of Dorothy, Principal Shairp, misunderstood), the fall of Corra Linn was one of the first objects they took pains to see, and the occasion gave rise to one of those metaphysical philological discussions in which Coleridge loved to share. A stranger on the scene observed that it was a "magnificent" waterfall. "Coleridge was delighted with the accuracy of the epithet," says Dorothy, which suggests that the term must have been less hackneyed and obvious then than now. He was particularly pleased, because he had "been settling in his own mind the precise meaning of the words grand, majestic, sublime, etc., and had discussed the subject with William at some length the day before. 'Yes, sir,' said Coleridge, 'it *is* a majestic waterfall.' 'Sublime and beautiful,' replied his friend. Poor Coleridge could make no answer, and, not very desirous to continue the conversation, came to us and related the story, laughing heartily." Perhaps it was the hour when the mistiest of metaphysicians was storing up rods in pickle for the Edinburgh School of Associationists, aesthetics who held that beauty, majesty and sublimity were only in the mind of man, and not intrinsic to the object seen; in other words, were "all my eye."

As a curious offset to the fact, which even Bain or Spencer would not controvert, that familiarity largely contributes to beauty, there is the fact that familiarity likewise breeds contempt, and waterfalls no longer attract the traveller off his good-going motor road, or count so much with him in his estimate of a holiday place as does the propinquity of a golf course. Falls in Britain are out of fashion, perhaps since Niagara and Victoria have created a standard that makes our grandest cataracts mere domestic water-taps by comparison; but still the Falls of Clyde have more than a local reputation, and they remain unspoiled, which is more than may be said of Niagara.

I fear, however, that, so far as the modern Scot is

KIRKFIELDBANK

concerned, his visit to the Falls is often but an afterthought, and is subservient to his going to the Lanark Races. One may, in the season, indulge conveniently the zest for starting-prices and the taste for cataracts by putting up at the county town, which still maintains much of its old-world charm, while conceding something to the modern preference for a good hotel, and in its neighbourhood are many of the most interesting features of the valley. Off the main line of railway, and half a mile from the river bank, Lanark nowadays dozes, and, passing through its vennels, lanes, "gates," "ports" and closes, that retain all the austerity, though they may have lost the squalor, of the middle ages, you can still hear the clack-clack of the hand-loom weaver's shuttle. A statue of Wallace dominates the High Street; the spirit of independence which he cherished is somehow even yet in the burgh's air, and no native thereof has been known to lose his passion for the place, however far he wandered. William Lithgow, to whom I have previously referred—a restless soul, who walked thirty-six thousand miles over Europe, the Levant, and Northern Africa, in the seventeenth century, and shared the tortures of the Spanish Inquisition, once stood by night in a creek of the Grecian Archipelago, dreading the attack of Turkish galliots, and composed a poem in which he prayed,

"Would God I might but live
  To see my native soil,
Twice happy is my happy wish
  To end this endless toil.

Yet still would I record
  The pleasant banks of Clyde,
Where orchards, castles, towns and woods
  Are planted side by side;
And chiefly Lanark, thou,
  Thy country's lowest lamp,
In which the bruised body now
  Did first receive the stamp."

It is not, perhaps, the pure gold of poetry, but it is eloquent of the true *maladie du pays* which always makes the exiled Scot a poet of sorts. He died, they say, in Lanark, and is buried in some unknown lair of the town's kirkyard, for "Lugless Will" (he had lost his ears in youth for an injudicious gallantry) was never in his life or death important enough to his own people to have a monument. He was certainly not important enough to be bowed to in Lanark Kirk by the clergyman, before beginning service, as some of the local gentry were. This custom once led to a bitter quarrel in the church, as two of the heritors disputed which of them should receive the first obeisance from the pulpit. At last the Presbytery held an inquiry into the circumstances, and came to the eminently sensible decision that there should be no more bowing to anyone.

To the ecclesiologist the ruins of St. Kentigern's church, dating back to the middle of the twelfth century, granted by David I. to the monks of Dryburgh, and continued in use till after the Reformation, will most appeal of all old Lanark's relics. Its bell,

THE CLYDE IN SPATE (NEAR LANARK)

reputed to be one of the oldest, if not the oldest, in Europe, and bearing an inscription that it had "three times, Phoenix-like, passed through fiery furnace, in 1110, 1659, and 1740," was transferred to the present Parish Church in 1777. To the archaeologist an artificial mound at the foot of the Castlegate is interesting, for it marks the site of a Roman station, and later of a royal castle. For the historian and patriot all the neighbourhood is redolent of Wallace, for here the War of Independence started, and his caves, that are as common in Scotland as the riven garments of Prince Charlie, or authentic portraits of Mary Stuart, are round about the Middle Ward in an embarrassing profusion.

A mile south of Lanark is New Lanark, a village which was the scene of one of the most ambitious attempts at practical communism ever made. A cotton mill was started here in 1783 by David Dale, and Arkwright, of the spinning-jenny; the waters of the Clyde were made to lend their power by way of a subterranean aqueduct through solid rock. Arkwright's association with an enterprise which resulted in the largest cotton spinning factory of the time, so far as Scotland was concerned, was brief, and Dale in turn disposed of the mills to Robert Owen, his son-in-law, who found in them the field for his philanthropic and socialistic experiments. Half a mile below is Braxfield, where the late Emperor Nicholas of Russia stayed on one occasion as the guest of Owen, studying (before his accession to the throne) democratic ideals from which Russia seems to be even yet remote; but there is, perhaps, more interest in the fact that Braxfield was the home of the hard-headed, hard-swearing, hard-hearted and hard-drinking old Scots judge who was the model for Stevenson's Weir of Hermiston.

Yet the roar of the linns allures from Lanark, new or old. They are still shut up in private grounds (though visible for a fee), as in the time of Wordsworth. Bonnington, the upper fall, and the least impressive, pours thirty feet into an abyss, to run for half a mile in furious rapids through a chasm seventy to a hundred feet deep. Corra Linn, with a fall almost three times higher, is less a fall than a series of cascades. The ruins of Corehouse Castle on its verge, and the cliffs encompassing, tremble in the thunder of the waters which Wordsworth apostrophised:

> "Lord of the Vale! astounding flood!
> The dullest leaf in this dark wood
> Quakes conscious of thy power:
>
> The caves reply with hollow moan,
> And vibrates to its central stone
> Yon time-cemented tower."

The scene, indeed, is marvellously impressive. Turner bathed his fancy in those swirling, rainbow-tinted canopies of spray, and produced a canvas that combines the minimum of natural fact with the maximum of ideal glamour in a fashion that has made it ever since a joy to the adept and a puzzle to the common man.

WALLACE'S LEAP (NEAR LANARK)

More solitary than either of the others, less popular with the multitude, and yet invested with peculiar charms, the fall of Stonebyres, two miles down from Lanark, is the broadest of the three, and was the barrier which the salmon which once escaped the pollution of Glasgow could never ascend. To see it at its best—as, indeed, to see any of the Falls of Clyde—is to see it in winter, part chained in flashing ice, its banks and woods snow-mantled.

Much of the appealing beauty of the river near Lanark is due to the tributary Mouse and Douglas. Douglasdale, alas! is outside of our survey, or it were sweet to linger for a while in that grey glen, in whose chapel lie the hearts of men, "tender and true" or otherwise—the Douglases. One is the heart of Archibald Bell-the-Cat, the other of that Good Sir James, who, bearing the heart of Bruce to the Holy Land, died on the frontiers of Granada, with a sentence on his lips that is like to remain the servant's ideal panegyric, the warrior's perfect vow.

Mouse Water, falling into the Clyde below Lanark, is more relevant to our theme. The last mile of its independence is at the bottom of a profound and romantic chasm known as the Cartland Crags. Dorothy Wordsworth called it a "rocky dell," and refused to think the Crags more wonderful than the Falls of Clyde; but her term is scarcely worthy, and the banks of the Mouse have associations with which she was unfamiliar. Though a sudden convulsion of the earth might seem to have occasioned this extraordinary cleft in the greywhack and red sandstone, or, as Scott has put it,

> "It seems some mountain rent and riven
> A channel for the stream had riven,"

it is really the gnawing work of the Mouse itself. For more than 400 feet on one side and 200 on the other, the cliffs, bearded with bush, tree and fern, brood over the dark and muddy water. A so-called Roman bridge makes up by its grace for the fact that, like all other "Roman bridges" in the country, it really belongs to a much later and more prosaic period. That Wallace, ere he went out to the slaying of the English sheriff at Lanark, hid himself in one of the caves here, is not impossible; and on the brink of the precipice is a spot called "Castle Qua," which yet shows traces of its ancient fortifications. But it is not the sound of strife we hear above the murmur of the stream that has flowed unchanged through all the centuries; it is the psalm of the Covenanters who hid and worshipped in these dim recesses.

WHERE THE MOUSE JOINS THE CLYDE

CHAPTER V

THE ORCHARD COUNTRY

It is in May that Clydesdale yields its deepest pleasure to the mind and eye. Then, to the wayfarer, the valley, full of flowers, and warm with an aromatic heat that seems to come from the earth rather than from the haze-hidden sun, has something foreign in its aspect and spirit. Were the Clyde broader, were the houses less geometrical, austere and grey, it might be a bit of Normandy, where the Seine lags under orchard trees between Rouen and Andelys. I know of nowhere else in Scotland like it; Scotland, indeed—land of brown heath and shaggy wood, grey cornfields, lonely glens, of sheep-folds, cots, and square farm-steadings set far apart in moors or grassy uplands—might be a million miles away, when from any of those high, ponderous bridges we look along the strath, and see the river linking through a world of orchards all in blossom. But I do not attach too much importance to the foreignness of the scene, for if the aesthetic emotions respond very rapidly to the beauty of places quite unlike the beauties among which we live, they exhaust themselves all the sooner, and we come back gladly to the typical features we know best, with fresher zest, to find that in them peculiarly lie all the finer, more abiding inspirations. Clydesdale is saved from being too exotic by something more than the remembrance that Wishaw is just round the Orchard Road, and that up the gorge of the Nethan pic-nic parties from Glasgow are shouting through the ruins of Tillietudlem Castle. The profounder deeps of the valley may be packed with berry bush and fruit tree, but you see the uplands are pure Scottish, as stern and monotonous as when the Covenanters held them, and over the sky-line on either hand of the valley you know there lie immediately the wide, unconquered moors, where the whaup whistles and the lapwing wheels and cries.

The charm of May in Clydesdale is mainly due to the orchard blossom, but it has origins deeper still. If all mankind loves a child, all mankind no less certainly loves a garden, and here is the greatest in our country, that stretches from Lanark almost to the confines of the parish of Blantyre. It was notable as such even in the eighth century, and the "appleyards of Lanark" find reference in the work of the venerable Bede. We go down from Wishaw upon Garrion Bridge, and cross to find ourselves in the thick of it. So much of Scotland lies waste, consecrate to ragweed, bracken, and heather, that if you did not try to buy it, you might think it the one thing in the country nobody set store by. It is not as in old lands like Italy, where each mountain terrace harbours a hamlet,

STONEBYRES FALLS

and cultivated vines sprawl up what here would be accounted inaccessible declivities. But in Clydesdale, along the river side, you will search in vain for ragweed. What soil can give root-room to a ragweed can accommodate a gooseberry bush. And the tiniest patches of ground, the steepest banks, the narrowest ravines that run into the river side are covered with berry plants or bushes, rasp cane, or plum and pear and apple trees. Strawberry beds are set diagonally across braes so steep that you wonder how the folk who weed and pick at them can keep a footing. Turning into the patch that leads up the Nethan, there are strawberries as wholly unprotected by fence or dyke from the passer-by as if they were potato rigs. A remarkable kind of small boy must be bred in Clydesdale, or is it that all boys there are early surfeited? Field after field shows green arches of rasp or marshalled rows of berry bushes. But on the fruit-trees only Clydesdale depends for her glory in May. Looking between the tall, clean, ancient beeches that shelter Millburn House on its pleasant eminence, or from the bridge at Garrion, the banks of Clyde appear festival with blossom. As you follow the road, then, up to Rosebank and Crossford, with its Cosy Glen, passing between an interminable succession of orchards, it is but natural to think that fruit-farming must be the ideal industry. Feeling yourself a mere wayfarer, as if you had got entry to one great garden through which the King's highway is a path and the river a cunning ornament, you may think the people blessed indeed whose lot it is to watch and guard the growth of things so clean, complete, beautiful in themselves, and universally acceptable as plums and pears, apples and berries. It might seem less a trade than a recreation, for if you have no delving and weeding to do yourself, a garden never suggests but leisure and indulgence.

But even into Clydesdale the primal curse has come. For all that these blossoming trees and fields of vine and berry suggest no thoughts but what are pleasant in this May morning for you who walk among them, hearing the cuckoo call in the woods of Mauldslie and Cambusnethan, and every orchard vocal with the songs of thrush and linnet, the folk whose whole fortune is in these sweet blossoms, and tender runners and emerald green arches, have other thoughts about them, and perhaps more anxieties than if they cultivated commoner things. A late frost, a stormy summer, that may merely discommode the grower of wheat and oats, may wholly spoil the fruit-farmer. And even if the seasons favour him, the very prodigality of nature may be his undoing, for he will suffer the influence of a glutted market. Years come now and then when the plums of Clydesdale are left to rot upon the trees, as it will not pay their owners to engage labour for their picking. It seems incredible, for there are millions wanting plums who cannot afford to buy them at their prices in the city shops, yet plum trees yield their fruit with but little care or cost. Behold, this thing is a great mystery! It is Economics; it is entangled

"TILLIETUDLEM" (CRAIGNETHAN CASTLE)

with problems of transit and labour and middlemen, whereof the wanderer through Clydesdale in May is blissfully ignorant. And there are, too, the men who manufacture preserves; 'tis said they combine at times, and come to an understanding that so much, and so much only, shall be the prevalent price for strawberries, and yet, again, the fruit-grower is in a cleft stick. No wonder the grower on a small scale is ever anxious, making less of a living for his labour than if he devoted his hours and powers to more prosaic farming. Only the owner of many acres, luckier if he be rent free, and with some skill in commerce, can achieve the respectability of a gig to drive him over the red roads of the neighbourhood. One crop only, and that of modern introduction, the Clydesdale fruit-farmer can depend on to return him a comparatively consistent reward for his time and labour—the tomato. Glass houses for the culture of the tomato are considerably increasing in numbers. They intrude, to some extent, a suggestion of mechanics, of the factory, for a series of tomato-houses, all architecturally designed for utility, and not for beauty, will mar the appearance of the most pleasant holm.

Clydesdale, however, would be attractive at this season even if there had been no more blossom than the gean tree gives. It is the most beautiful part of Lanarkshire, and is outside the radius of steel works, with long vistas wholly unspoiled by the sight of chimney stacks. The banks swell up from the river in graceful billows. The river itself loiters and bends as if reluctant to leave so fine a place behind it. There are woods that rise high up on the hill sides, and a sufficiency of stately homes among the trees to give a hint of history and romance. The history and romance are less in the present dwellings, however, than in their situations, for Mauldslie Castle dates no further back than 1793, though its site in the days of Baliol was the centre of a royal forest; and Milton Lockhart, on its peninsula, backed by deep ravines and wooded hills, owes its greatest interest, apart from its natural beauty, to the fact that Scott chose the site of its mansion for the half-brother of his son-in-law and biographer. Lee Castle, nearer Lanark, boasts a more obvious connection with the past, for it stands upon foundations that were laid when the Caledonian Forest was in its prime. The "Lee-Penny" is still there, its power to cure the ills of man and beast no longer put to the test in a sceptical age. There is little about Dalserf to indicate its ancient story, when it was appendage and chapelry of Cadzow, and the property alternately of the Comyns and the Crown. The Comyns plainly knew a good thing when they saw it; this rich little piece of land in a link of the river has a peculiar charm. We walk through its churchyard, to find it trim, and swept of all intelligible records of its past, the only literature afforded by its tombstones apparently being a rhyming epitaph on a Covenanter who fought the good fight, but died prosaically in bed.

No, it is not in mansions, kirks, or tombs, or even in her pretty villages that Clydesdale in this part has

CRAIGNETHAN FARM

her peculiar attractiveness; that seems to depend most on the presence of the river. So it must be, at all events, for the anglers, whom we see on this benign May morning, standing on jutting points of the bank, or wading waist-deep in the stream. They are so numerous, they ply their gentle craft so assiduously for most part of the year, that however satisfactory the aggregate catch may be, the sport for the individual must be more ruminative than exciting. Even up the Nethan, before it has joined the Clyde at Crossford, we find the industrious Waltonian, child of hope. The hanging woods are full of melody, the air is soft and faintly perfumed; the river sings, and it is on a wonderfully noble prospect the walls of Craignethan look down. Scott, who invested these ruins with the romance of his imagination, and sent the visitor ever since looking for certain windows and trees that were probably purely windows and trees of the mind, "swithered" when offered a part of Tillietudlem for his dwelling. It was, indeed, a tempting opportunity if the month was May.

CHAPTER VI

BY CASTLED CRAGS

THAT the landlords on Tweedside should have lately decided upon closing a long stretch of that classic water to the angler—though only temporarily, let us hope—naturally roused the apprehensions of West Coast anglers, who have immemorially plied their art and craft on the upper reaches of the Clyde; for if Tweed trout may be so preserved, why not the trout of the Clyde, which may sometimes, as tradition says, be spawned in the same burns?

> "From one vast mountain bursting on the day,
> Tweed, Clyde, and Annan urge their separate way,"

according to the poet Wilson of "The Clyde." Michael Scott, the wizard, once threatened by his unco art, of which nowadays we may be permitted to be sceptical, to cut a channel by which the waters of our western stream should flow for ever after into Tweed. Sir Archibald Geikie, as I have already shown, has degraded the Clyde of the glacial period to a mere tributary of that other Scottish stream, which has,

CROSSFORD FROM THE ORCHARDS

perhaps, had more than its fair share of the glamour that comes from poetry and romance more often than from Nature's charms. It is said—I know not with what truth, if truth be in it—that at certain seasons floods near Biggar affect a sort of Meredithian marriage between both rivers, and that the rare presence of a sea-trout or salmon in the upper Clyde presumes some offspring of the union, since no such fish could survive the passage of the Broomielaw, even if they could scale the falls at Lanark. At all events, the humble angler of the West must have felt alarmed to see a correspondent lately make the bold suggestion that in the interest of real sport such drastic measures as have been taken on the Tweed were called for on the Clyde from Crawford to Carstairs. There were in his communication dark innuendoes of illegal methods on the part of the humbler brethren of the angle who come at night from Wishaw, Bellshill, Bothwell, Hamilton, and Motherwell, and return at morn with a suspicious number of well-filled baskets for a sparse proportion of rods.

Well, I have fished the upper Clyde—in a manner of speaking, for it was often fishing in the apostolic sense, since no fish were forthcoming. I have spent bland and starry summer nights on the banks at Symington and Culter, and started wading at dawn on stretches of the river that seemed to have more fishers to the mile than any other stream in Scotland, and it was perhaps my unsophistication that led me to see or suspect nothing mala-fide. There are Clydeside anglers who are said to make a living by what for the rest of us is a not inexpensive recreation, among them, alas! no more, the talented and entertaining author of "The Angler and the Loop Rod." David Webster, year in, year out, kept up a marvellously constant supply of Clyde trout for one of the Glasgow fishmongers. But careful scrutiny of my fellow-anglers and of their baskets by day and night in this district have led me to believe that, so far from there being a living in the fish of upper Clyde, there is rarely a decent breakfast, and if illegal methods are employed, it must be very seldom. It is long since I ceased to display my own inefficiency as Piscator on a river that demands very cunning fishing; but all my sympathies are still with the humble sportsmen who, wading waist-deep in the curves of Culter, or casting under banks in the shadow of Tinto, give Clyde, on a summer or autumn day, a human and cheerful aspect. They give, in their presence, the last touch needed to suggest a sad comparison of those wild, beautiful, unspoiled waters with what is their ultimate destiny—the degradation of the drain-pipe, the slime of works, the bondage to a commerce that can flourish only on the ruins of God's gifts. It is fitting, too, I think, that here the Clyde should be the people's; it is virtually all that is left them whereon to practise lures essentially the same as were used by those old children of the chase who whipped the river when the wild Caledonian bull crashed through the surrounding pines.

Going back with those colliers and ironworkers from

NETHANFOOT

the banks of the pellucid river to the towns that are their homes, you would be churlish indeed to grudge them their brief hours at a sport, which, more than any other that survives among their class, must be pursued in clean and peaceful scenes, and under circumstances that engender quiet and contemplation. Witnessing those squadrons of rod-bearers detraining in the gloomy railway stations, and plunging into a night smoke-laden, or sinister with leaping fires, they seem as worthy as those conquerors of Breda whose lances rank in the picture of Velasquez. They go back from the linking river and the song of birds and the Scotland of a thousand years ago to where modern Scotland is digging her luxurious living from the entrails of the earth, and welding her own chains with mighty hammers. When the streets of Hamilton and Motherwell are foul with the mud of the toilers' feet on a winter night, and the black rain falls, there must often be anglers at the corners thinking of a "bonny wind and a braw water" on the heights behind. They are still within sound of the romantic river, which ends only at Bothwell; but here it is not theirs, and they are too far from Elvanfoot to emulate the old baker who for half-a-century was a familiar figure on the side of Clyde. It was a common thing for him, after a hard day's work, to walk eight miles through the hills to the river, fish till after midnight, and walk back and start his day's work again. On one occasion he did this and caught nothing. But during the intervals of work next day he made a new cast of flies, repeated his journey, and this time was rewarded with a heavy basket. Again he started home, and got there only in time to start his third day's work without sleep.

All that saves the Scottish "Black Country" from the most hopeless degradation—artistically speaking—is the presence of the Clyde, with what survives of old grandeur that gathered there in other ages. It was, undoubtedly, the natural beauty and fertility of the strath which borders the broad and rushing waterway, the felicitous accidents of curve, vista, holm, thicket, and ravine, the extensive natural parks, and the happy shelter, that accounted most for the presence there of those stately homes that bear the name of Blantyre, Hamilton, and Dalzell. Dorothy Wordsworth, when she drove leisurely with her brother along those roads, more than a hundred years ago, discovered in Hamilton Palace "a large building without grandeur, a heavy, lumpish mass"; and Thomas Gray, of the "Elegy," thought it a "great ill-contrived edifice" when he came on it in his tour in Scotland in 1764. But the palace has been vastly altered since then, and may safely claim to be one of the finest in the kingdom. A small square tower of very ancient date formed the nucleus of the oldest part of the present palace, erected about 1591, added to in 1705-17, and given its present grandiose proportions only in 1822. Its environment has an idyllic beauty that not even a race-course crowd can mar—for Hamilton Park is Glasgow's Epsom—yet somehow

A FAVOURITE POOL (NEAR ROSEBANK)

the glory of Hamilton house seems nowadays a little wilted when we remember its ravishing by the auctioneer of 1882. Four hundred thousand pounds were got for its art and bibliographic treasures, and there is little doubt that had the sale taken place to-day that figure would have been more than doubled. Wordsworth composed an indifferent sonnet on the gem of the collection, Rubens' "Daniel in the Lion's Den," which sold for £5,145, but is now restored to its old place among a very charming group of family portraits by some of the greatest English masters.

For the bibliophile, the tragedy of Hamilton Palace lies in the dispersal of its Beckford Library, founded by the author of "Vathek," whose daughter married Duke Alexander. Its 15,000 volumes, amongst which were many rare editions of the early authors, along with Duke Alexander's library, comprised together 25,000 volumes and 800 volumes of MSS.

While the palace, as I think, holds (of course in a less degree) the pathos of Versailles and Holyrood, despite the fact that in its present state it is mostly modern, and has sheltered only casual royalties, not even the smuts of the "Black Country" can mar the splendour of the policies, or rob us of the sentiment that haunts old Cadzow Forest. That the white cattle still roaming there are real descendants of the wild herds that bred in the forest of Caledonia I prefer to believe, in spite of expert assurance that they are only an ancient domesticated breed. Cadzow Castle itself, far older than Robert the Bruce, perched high on its rocky pinnacle over the Avon, mantled by ivy, lulled in the sleep of age by the murmuring stream; and the Mausoleum, built by Duke Alexander at a cost of £130,000, with superb bronze doors, that are more or less replicas of the celebrated gates of Ghiberti in the Baptistery of Florence, are memorials of the most solemn achievement of the first and of the latest of the Hamiltons. Cadzow Castle, silent, simple, strong, where

> "The glimmering spears are seen no more,
> The shouts of war die on the gales,
> Or sink in Avon's lonely roar,"

truly ministers to the pensive mood, while the Mausoleum, with its Ghiberti gates, and Memphian sarcophagus, echoing oft to the visitor's psalm (specially recommended by the cicerone), affects the sentimentalist as little as if he were in the Invalides listening to Cook's guide lecture on the tomb of Napoleon.

Beautiful though the woods and parks of Hamilton are—they are seen at their best, perhaps, in the pictures of Sam Bough and Alexander Fraser—one's heart warms more to Bothwell Castle, possibly the finest ruin of its kind in Scotland,

> "Where once proud Murray, Clydesdale's ancient lord,
> A mimic sovereign, held the festal board."

In an old book of 1605—Verstegan's "Restitution of Decayed Intelligence"—an incident is narrated which should touch the heart of any Clydesdale man. It runs as follows:—"So fell it out of late years that an

MAULDSLIE CASTLE

English gentleman, travelling in Palestine, not far from Jerusalem, as hee passed through a country towne, hee heard by chance a woman sitting at her doore dandling her childe to sing 'Bothwel bank thou blumest fayre.' The gentleman heereat exceedingly wondered and forthwith, in English, saluted the woman, who joyfully answered him, and told him that she was a Scottish woman." That three-century-old song may well have been inspired by the sweep of the great declivity over which hangs the castle where English kings have slept, finding "Bothwell bank" at last a little grudging in its hospitality. Ivy, wild rose, and wallflower cover old Bothwell, making a kindly veil for its decay. Blantyre Priory, on the opposite bank of the river, founded for Austin canons in 1296, seems to be an echo of its sentiment of sad romance. Each lends the other a peculiar grace, and the river, running deep and silent underneath, may at witched midnight surely hear some strange reminiscences. According to tradition, its waters still flow over a vaulted passage which formerly connected the two ruins, a feature of which Miss Jane Porter properly makes the most in her "Scottish Chiefs." Dalzell House, a seventeenth century house on the site of a peel of great antiquity, has a Roman camp on its grounds, through which passed the Roman highway of Watling Street. But I prefer my castles on cliffs, as at Craignethan, Cadzow, and Bothwell, and I quickly pass from Dalzell to the magic gardens of Barncluith, whose old Dutch terraces, 250 feet above the swirling and wood-mantled Avon, once seen on an autumn afternoon or walked through in moonshine, during "the rare and welcome silence of the snow," are never to be forgotten. Barncluith is, of all the ancient dwellings in that romantic neighbourhood, the one which should most bewitch the angler; it was so obviously built for peace and an artistic eye and the propinquity of good fishing, while all the others were built for war.

And then there is Bothwell Brig, where the romance of Clydesdale finds its consummation—the mute memorial span (renovated in 1826) which Hackston of Rathillet and Hall of Haughead held with 300 Covenanters against the trained troops of Monmouth only long enough to make the onset of the Royalists the more infuriated, and the subsequent shock of battle on the green behind more fatal for "unworthy Robin Hamilton" and the 4,000 insurgent saints, whose internal disagreements made such a sad *dénouement* quite inevitable.

BROOMIELAW, GLASGOW

CHAPTER VII

NEARING THE CITY

HAVING, in our journey down the river, passed Bothwell, against whose sandstone terraces the waves of an estuary onetime doubtless beat, we can no longer conceal from ourselves the saddening fact that the Clyde is swiftly approaching its prosaic and squalid interlude, as it must seem, at least, to all who, like Thomas Campbell, count it no improvement

> ". . . to have changed
> My native Clyde, thy once romantic shore
> Where nature's face is banished and estranged
> And Heaven reflected in thy wave no more."

We may still stand on banks that are fragrant with wild-flower and vocal with bird-song and the chuckle of the stream among the boulders, but on the rise of the valley to the right we see uplift at no great distance dreadful and sinister columns, factory chimneys set as close as trees, and always over them a cloud by day, or by night the pulsing glow of Tophet. It is Scotland's "Black Country"; 180 square miles of coal outcrop are in Lanarkshire, and you cannot wander very far from the river in this neighbourhood without hearing the oppressive pant of a coal-pit engine. Our neighbourhood, too, is the most prominent iron-producing district in the country; at one time it was first in Britain, and is second now only to Cleveland. Half a hundred blast furnaces blow almost within hearing of each other —Langloan, Gartsherrie, Coltness, Calder, Clyde, Wishaw, Carnbroe, Shotts, Summerlee and Mossend. Huge fortunes have been made in the industry since David Mushet, of the Clyde Iron Works, in 1801 discovered that the material which the miners were rejecting under the name of "wild coal" was a valuable iron ore, to which the name blackband ironstone has been given, and since Beaumont Neilson introduced the hot blast at the same place. Lanark, however, can no longer depend on her own insufficient supply of ores; the rise of the mild steel industry in 1872 has led to enormous importation of red and brown iron ores from different parts of the world. Over twenty years ago it looked as if the malleable iron industry which followed close on the manufacture of pig-iron was on the verge of extinction through the increasing competition of mild steel, but Coatbridge, Motherwell, and Wishaw yet thrive and grow, fed mainly on the output of a score of mills or forges, where steam-hammers thud perpetually, and puddles continually fill with what looks like liquid gold.

Here we have nothing to do with them, since, though obvious in their influence on the air and sky, and even on the character of the populace, which is no longer pastoral to the eye, idyllic to the ear, they are far enough apart from the banks of Clyde to call for no more than passing reference. We shall follow the winding of the river past pleasant enough but commonplace Uddingston to Kenmuir Woods and Carmyle. Kenmuir and Carmyle—alas! they are not what they were when they first drew wedding parties to its "bonnie well" and the latter was the haunt of angler, artist and lover. Horatio M'Culloch, Docharty, Milne Donald, Sam Bough, Alexander Fraser, M'Whirter, George Reid, and many other notable painters of the Scottish school sometime or other pitched their easels by Carmyle and Kenmuir; the silver stream below its steep and wooded banks, and the sylvan cloisters that made a sort of Arden for our grandfathers, and that old men speak of still wistfully as places fairy and memory-haunted, as in a sense the last of Glasgow's idyllic outskirts, have a charm on many canvases that must preserve for us the unspoiled spirit of these places when the last remnant of their glory is gone, as it quickly goes.

Then comes Cambuslang, to the east of which is a spacious natural amphitheatre, which was in 1742 the scene of one of the most astounding religious revivals ever known—the "Cambuslang Wark," where the great Calvinistic Methodist, George Whitefield, with a band of clergy, held, day after day, in the words of Hill Burton, "a festival which might be called awful, but scarcely solemn, among a multitude calculated by contemporary writers to amount to 30,000 people." In Cambuslang, with the trolley cars of the city clanging through its streets, its air impregnated with the odour of brewery draff and dyeworks or the smuts from a myriad steel and iron-works about it, the Clyde grown dingy, Tinto may seem a dream; but we have only to climb 600 feet to the top of Dechmont, on the north of the town, to see again the lord of the Upper Ward, to whose beacon fires those of Dechmont once responded.

Tortuously the river shifts and doubles after leaving Cambuslang, as if reluctant to meet its fate in the murky city; but too soon Rutherglen claims it—the hour has come!

Ru'glen we call it, and must have always called it, in our indolent western way, which makes Milguy of Milngavie, and is perhaps something more than a lazy make-shift, being further, I imagine, a symptom of affection, as diminutives are in Christian names. It was the delight of a worthy old Glasgow cleric of the last century, Dr. Hately Waddell, to discover in the place-names from Bothwell to Glasgow purely maritime derivations, which would show, as the fossil sea-shells found all over Clydesdale do perhaps more obviously, that the Firth or Fiord of Clyde at one time covered the present land from Kilpatrick to the Gleniffer Braes, from Jordanhill to Camphill, from Garnethill to Cathkin Braes, and from Camlachie Ridge to Bothwell. Dr. Waddell concluded that Rutherglen was Rudha-iar-glen, a crabbed sort of Gaelic for the "point of the west valley," which, for his argument, was a valley running into the Clyde. With a confidence which is enviable he pictured Cambuslang ("the bay of ships" by his philology) as the main harbour of the ancient firth, "which might often be as much crowded with the primitive craft of the river as Bowling Bay now is with disabled steamers or Gourock Bay with yachts and pleasure boats for hire." As the firth receded, trade, he held, would recede also, and ships of a sort that once sheltered in Cambuslang would be reduced at last to the necessity of mooring at Rutherglen. It is a pretty speculation, nor is the vital part of it—the argument that Rutherglen was once a port of sorts—without evidence more convincing. Rutherglen's coat of arms, as impressed on the most ancient charters of the corporation, bears prominently the figure of a ship, which may have been only the *Navis antiqua* of heraldry signifying that the town stood on a river more or less navigable, as folk jealous of Ru'glen's old reputation argue, but the Clyde was undoubtedly open to ships of light draft as far up as Rutherglen at no very remote period, and before the Clyde Navigation Acts were passed in 1750, and before the Broomielaw Bridge was built in 1768, there were frequently more vessels to be seen at the quay of Rutherglen than at Glasgow. Probably they were not argosies of much importance to the wider mercantile world—mostly Highland wherries or flat-bottomed barges laden with herring from Lochfyne, ling-fish, eggs, farm produce, or coals—but there they were, and Ru'glen claims paternity from the wave with as much right as the "sea-born city" three miles further down.

What is indisputable is that Rutherglen was a Royal Burgh, with its provost and bailies, long before Glasgow was anything more than a mere village, governed by its bishop. In 1126, in the reign of David I., it was erected into a burgh, with the privileges of trade for a wide district, extending on the west to the river Kelvin, and embracing, apparently, the town of Glasgow and that part of "Perdeyc" (Partick) which was situated on the east side of the Kelvin. Its magistrates lifted toll or custom within the territory of Glasgow, and this practice seems to have been continued even after Glasgow had been made a bishop burgh by King William in 1175-1178. On 29th October, 1226, King Alexander directed the Rutherglen bailies not to take toll or custom within the town of Glasgow, but authorised them to continue the collection of such dues "at the cross of Schedinstun, as they were wont to be taken of old." Schedinstun—now known as Shettleston—is on the north side of the Clyde, which shows that Rutherglen territory at that time extended beyond the river. Yet Rutherglen relinquished her claims on the barony of Glasgow reluctantly, for two centuries later King James had again to interdict her putting a tariff on the trade of her neighbour town.

There is little about Rutherglen to-day that suggests its old importance as the chief town in Lower Lanarkshire, a predominance it held as late as the fifteenth century. No stone remains of its ancient castle, which was strongly garrisoned by the English during the War of Independence, besieged several times by Robert the Bruce, and eventually taken by his brother Edward in 1313. Only the quaint old steeple remains of the church within whose walls a truce between Scotland and her "auld enemy" was arranged in 1297, and where Sir John Menteith—if Blind Harry may be "lippened to"—engaged to betray Wallace for English gold. On the anniversary of the Restoration in May, 1679, the burghers of Rutherglen, less Radical then than now, apparently, celebrated the event by kindling a bonfire in the chief street of the town. A band of Covenanters, led by Hackston, Burleigh, and Hamilton, rode in to trample out the bonfire, and, after psalm and prayer, affixed on Ru'glen Cross a public protest against the proceedings of the Government, committing to the flames of a bonfire of their own all the Acts of the Scottish Parliament that had been passed in favour of Prelacy. It was the start of the rebellion, as Claverhouse surmised. Some of his troopers watched these proceedings from a discreet distance; next day he was in pursuit of the rebels, to meet more than his match in the bogs of Drumclog.

Such are some of the historical associations of the old town, whose "wee round red lums reek briskly" still, but which, till it became a suburb of Glasgow, was for long to be known as little more than a weaving hamlet. That Rutherglen declined as Glasgow swelled in power and place is a phenomenon which has been variously accounted for; doubtless there were a thousand inter-relating causes that made the change inevitable. Glasgow, a close burgh, ruled by the bishops till the seventeenth century, and for long thereafter by self-elected merchants, held the mercantile interest always paramount, and had a prescient eye for the possibilities of the river as a highway to her fortunes, while Ru'glen, with its popular elections and other privileges, spent its public enthusiasm on purely local and evanescent disputes. It is a curious comment on Democracy. During the reign of Mary, the townsmen of Glasgow, Renfrew and Dumbarton joined forces to work six weeks at the removal of a formidable sandbank across the river at Dumbuck, and make other improvements. Rutherglen, whose interest in such an operation was just as great as that of any of them, took no part in the work. In 1755, when the magistrates of Glasgow consulted Smeaton about the deepening of the Clyde, Rutherglen again stood back. It may have been that by then the destiny of Glasgow was too obvious, or the resources of a community that was now the smallest of the royal burghs were too small. All that associates her now with maritime affairs is Seath's ship-building yard. The hand-loom has departed from her lanes and tenements; she is redolent of dye-works, rope-yards and chemical works; while brick-fields, collieries, potteries and iron-works limit most of her horizon.

Not wholly, however. About a mile and a half south of Rutherglen are Cathkin Braes, which, through

KINGSTON DOCK, GLASGOW

the munificence of a Glasgow man—Mr. James Dick —were presented to the city on condition that they should be left in their natural state. Six hundred feet above the sea level, they command a noble view of the valley of the Clyde, the mountains of Argyll and Arran, and the still more distant Arthur's Seat and Pentland Hills. Cathkin Braes extend to about fifty acres, and are richly clothed with natural wood, bracken, and broom. The highest point on the estate is called Queen Mary's Seat, from which it is said she watched the overthrow of her final hopes at the battle of Langside.

CHAPTER VIII

GLASGOW

"To describe a city so much frequented as Glasgow is unnecessary," said Dr. Johnson—so providing the evidence that one journalistic way of getting out of a difficulty was as well known in the eighteenth century as it is in Fleet Street to-day. No city, in truth, is to be described to the stranger in a dozen Johnsonian paragraphs; no stranger may discover, in a brief visit to any city, the parts of it that are really of importance, the features that peculiarly endear it to its residents, or give it at least an almost human personality in their affections or dislikes—its shy, domestic, intimate, communal life. That is of far more importance than statistics, imposing buildings, splendid streets, squares, and historical remains, but it is his eyes alone the casual visitor generally brings to the appraisement of any new city whereunto he has entered with expectation, perhaps with prejudices and foregone conclusions, and it is likely that in most instances he will depart from such a city as Glasgow without for a moment feeling the influence of that elusive and precious thing the *genius loci*, its essential and intimate atmosphere that is discoverable only to the long resident, who sees warm, hospitable lights at night through the smoke of furnaces, and can invest the most thunderous thoroughfare, the most dreary vista of tenements, with memories and associations more poignant than he could bring from the Acropolis or muster within him a year after a Cook's tour to Venice.

For your first and last impression of a city like Glasgow much depends on what you seek, on the variety of your interests and the width of your sympathies. It is, for instance, no place for the single-minded enthusiast whose passion is trout-fishing or the collection of birds' eggs. Yet it is vastly more than a huge workshop, where wheels eternally hum, and shrewd men at a bargain haggle over counters and desks. Though it is, as it were, a growth of the nineteenth century, yet its roots are deep in history, and some of its streets have heard the sounding hoofs of armies and looked on the passing of old kings and queens. We have little left in stone and lime, beyond the Cathedral, to prove it, but Glasgow is of an antiquity as picturesque and romantic as it is almost incredible to one who sees it to-day without the knowledge of the historian or the eye of imagination.

A mighty place for trade—so the English drummer tells us—strenuous, hard-working, shrewd and "canny," with what to the Southern, who does not know, may seem a lack of gaiety; with a stern and arid Sabbath; and a preposterous early hour for the closing of public houses. Yet others have discovered therein a certain rugged hospitality, and it has even been credited with a sense of humour—two virtues, the recognition and appreciation of which will help the stranger within its gates the better to understand it.

In a couplet of Mr. Kipling's poem "M'Andrew's Hymn," he has practically set the limits of the city's civic activity—

> "From Maryhill to Pollokshaws,
> From Govan to Parkhead."

Northward, where rises the enormous chimney stalk of St. Rollox, the hurried visitor need not take the trouble to penetrate, unless he be interested in the production of chemicals or locomotives, that go to the far ends of the earth. Nor need he go further east than Gallowgate and the old Cathedral if it is entertainment for the eye and the imagination he is after. South of the river he shall find parks and gardened suburbs and even hills, if he take the trouble to step upon the right tramway car, and have the essential penny; and west he may go anywhere and be singularly unfortunate if he does not come upon much that should please him. For as it is from east to west, from the broad and generous bosom of Strathclyde, our river flows through dingy purlieus to the clean and sovereign sea, so westward, as in most cities, lie all Glasgow's aspirations and most of her operations towards refinement, purity, beauty and peace.

Yet Glasgow, squatted, in her business parts, upon

what was once swampy river banks, is fortunate, too, in being largely set upon hills, and from any eminence in the very heart of her you can—given a decent day—see other and higher hills engirdling her. The mountain winds blow on her from the Campsies and the Mearns; at her very doors are innumerable pathways to the wilds. There is a hackneyed and cynical epigram about Glasgow's privileges in this respect that need not be here repeated, but the visitor shall have overlooked a vital fact in regard to Glasgow as a city to live in, if he does not know that in thirty-five or forty minutes' journey by rail from the centre of the city, he may find himself before the unparalleled beauty of the Firth of Clyde, on the shores of the Queen of Scottish Lakes, in moorland fastnesses, or in lonely hamlets of the hills.

Before he goes there, however, let him see what he can of the city of St. Mungo. The arteries of her pulsate at the exit from the railway stations—Argyle Street, more antique and active than elegant nowadays, alas! Buchanan Street, among whose shops ladies love to loiter of an afternoon; Renfield Street, consecrate to warehouses and offices and the ceaseless ding-dong of trolley cars; Jamaica Street, portal to the Broomielaw and the river, with its "earnest of romance"; George Square—Ah! George Square, for its condition we would tender a thousand apologies. To the discriminate it is enough that George Square is often called the Valhalla—an allusion to its statues whereof there is a weird embarrassment. At no time so elegant or important as a central "place" in a city like Glasgow should be, George Square to-day is often in a singular and piteous deshabille. Should you love monuments, they are there and unavoidable.

Towering to the east of George Square, with somewhat fretful front but ever hospitable doors, are the city's Municipal Buildings, in which the affairs of this great community are administered, and notably well administered, as the stranger may judge almost as well as the ratepayer. A Lord Provost and seventy-six Magistrates and Town Councillors, including two representatives of the city's ancient Trades and Guilds, who sit *ex officio*, here labour for love of the city with a disinterestedness for which they sometimes get grudging credit; in these chambers is the official mechanism of Glasgow, in the Banqueting Hall is the scene of the more important civic hospitalities.

The police supervision of the city, the provision of gas and electric light, of water from far-off mountain lochs in the silent, heather-scented, deer-frequented Highland hills; the management of the tram-car system, that radiates far into the country, and even into other and older towns than Glasgow; of public parks and open spaces, free libraries, baths, picture galleries, museums, halls, and many churches, the cleansing of the streets—all these depend upon the shrewdness, the business acumen and integrity of the city's elected representatives who sit in the Municipal Buildings.

From the central bureau of these modern activities to Glasgow's most ancient possession, the Cathedral,

QUEEN'S DOCK, GLASGOW (N. BASIN)

French barque "Cannebière" unloading cargo of nickel ore from New Caledonia

is but a short tram-car journey. There are people in Glasgow itself who boast that they have never seen this worthiest, noblest ecclesiastical monument in their midst; theirs is the loss, although in truth there is a slight excuse to be found for them in the unattractiveness of its environment. Itself an erection of the twelfth century, it stands on the site of a much older edifice dedicated to St. Mungo, Glasgow's patron saint. Once its bell rang over a pure and peaceful little valley by the gorge of a sweet, clean stream, the Molendinar, now degraded to the status of a drain-pipe, and mercifully hid, and the wild-birds sang more gaily than they do to-day in the hill beside it—the tall Necropolis, whose tomb-encumbered summit looks so strange against the eastern sky. The exterior of the Cathedral may disappoint, but to the discerning its crypt or under church, the finest in Britain, will always appeal with the force of perfect art, and its dim, cool depths will never fail to stimulate a healthy imagination. Round the Cathedral, or rather between it and the river Clyde, in a narrow strip of land, whose streets and lanes still bear their old eloquent appellations, grew old Glasgow, and in the High Street, till comparatively recent years, was situate the College of Glasgow, founded four and a half centuries ago. It had become no place, the High Street, for academic groves; squalor and vice and crime had come where once walked holy men and decent, prosperous burgesses, and the present University of Glasgow was built to the West of the city in 1867-70, at a cost of more than half a million sterling.

We have not, it is true, in any part of Glasgow, the entrancing views that some parts of Edinburgh afford, but Gilmorehill, on which the University stands, gives a prospect we may be pardoned for looking on with some complacency. The architecture of the building itself has been called in question as unsuitable for the summit of an eminence, where innumerable little turrets mar the effect of dignity and consummation a long, low, classic structure would have better sustained. This criticism has no application, however, when one is beside the walls themselves, and looking down upon the hill slopes on Kelvingrove, the city's West End Park, the river Kelvin crashing over its weirs, the new Art Galleries, opened in 1901, the mansions, churches, steeples, and towers that lie south of the classic steep, and lose themselves, alas! too often, in the haze before the eye has reached the swelling uplands of the Mearns. It is here, perhaps, more than other places in Glasgow, that its thoughtful citizens realise the mightiness of the heart that beats in her, and dream of the greatness of her destiny. No, commerce is not Glasgow's god, nor its poor fleeting rewards her only stimulant; handmaiden among the cities of Britain, drudge and serf, that the wide world may be gay in the fabrics of her making, and safely sail the ocean in her honest ships, or speed in security and comfort in many lands behind her iron horses, and trust the integrity of her metal and the skill of her working men, Glasgow vividly or vaguely sees her future in the ampler horizons that encircle Gilmorehill. Thence still flows the same clear stream of learning, of culture, of righteous endeavour that had its first source in the old High Street College, four hundred years and a half ago. In all the later years of her strenuous toil and its inevitable grime, she has not all forgotten that while the Molendinar, by whose pure purling water our forefathers played, is a ditch, and buried, her way lies west, in the course of a nobler stream, that flows into a land of golden evenings.

The Clyde!—it has been Glasgow's highway to fortune, as it is to so many of her people the highway home to the hills and the shores they came from. She made it herself what it is out of a shallow, narrow salmon stream, where cobbles precariously navigated; robbed it of its pellucid and pastoral charms, and in a century turned it, as has been aptly said, to "a tide in the affairs of men." To-day it is not lovely to the eye (or even to the nose) of the enthusiast who has come to Glasgow for trout-fishing or the collection of the aforesaid eggs, but it is, let us remember, still but in the making. While we admire the Titan energy thundering on the rivets of its shipbuilding yards, and wonder to see great battle-ships, and argosies from every land, come and go through miles of pasture land and wharf to and from this inland city, we willingly forget the spoiling of the salmon stream; the more readily because we know the Clyde is, as has been said, but in the making even yet, and the purification of it has already been begun.

CHAPTER IX

WHARF AND DOCK

In the old days, the Clyde, having poured its flood narrowly, deeply, and picturesquely through that part of its valley I have already dealt with, found margins less constricting when it came to the plain that is now filled up with the streets of Glasgow. There it widened out, shallow and sluggish, between indefinite and broken banks, filtering itself of the detritus it has brought down from the hills; bereft of its young impetuous urge, its passion spent. The little town of Glasgow lay on its northern bank; on the south side cattle grazed upon a swampy area into which the Clyde at floods intruded, an erratic and unwelcome visitor. Wayward waters from the stream stole round sandy islets; there was one between the city and the Gorbals, which disappeared in 1754, and west of the Kelvin there were half-a-dozen whose memory still survives in the single instance of Whiteinch. In the middle ages the course of the river was doubtless more definite and its channel deeper than in later years, for we know that in the reign of Malcolm Ceannmor a fleet of 160 ships "landed at Renfriu," with Somerled's invading army, and if Fordun's chronicle may be trusted, King Alexander brought up safely at Glasgow with a fleet and army mustered to subdue the territory of Argyll. Herrings came up in silver shoals as far as Renfrew, and were fished for there, the monks of Holyrood in the twelfth century having a charter from King David to net them when they could.

But the silt of the river at and below Glasgow rendered it practically unnavigable for all save the smallest kind of vessels in the seventeenth century, and a hundred years later the depth of water in the harbour was only fourteen inches at low tide and at its highest did not exceed 3½ feet. The commercial value of their waterway had been too long overlooked by the people of the neighbourhood, who doubtless saw in it merely the possibilities of trout and salmon fishing, rights to which went with the leases of their "tofts" and gardens, and it seemed a hopeless state of affairs they had to face when in 1662, having found Dumbarton unwilling to be their port on the canny grounds that the presence of too many mariners would raise the cost of food to the inhabitants, they began to "make the Clyde."

They had in 1566 laboured at the removal of the formidable sandbank at Dumbuck; in 1662 the Magistrates and Town Council of Glasgow as River and Harbour Authority, decided "for many guid reasons and considerations, for the more commodious laidining and landing of boats, that there be ane little key builded at the Broomielaw, and that the samyn be done and perfectit with the best convenience be sight and advys of the magistrates Deane of Gild and Deacon Conveiner." It extended above what is now the site of Glasgow Bridge, and was apparently a structure of stone, but was faced with wood, and there is a Gothic bluntness too typical, I fear, of early Glasgow, about the instructions given to the Dean of Guild in the following year to use oaken timber from the Cathedral for alterations on the pier. Even with the aid of ecclesiastical oak it was a wretched and inadequate thing and had to be supplanted by a better one in 1688, at a cost of £1600. On the whole, it did not matter much; vessels—all but the merest shallops—could not come nearer than fourteen miles, and cargo had to be conveyed from there or from Port Glasgow, east of Greenock, to the Broomielaw in flat bottomed barges of three or four tons burthen. In the century which followed, Glasgow grasped at the tobacco trade, and the ships she owned began to venture into strange seas, but they never saw the city, for the old unconquered shoal at Dumbuck kept them from the upper reaches, which were still in a state of nature in 1755. There were then, in the 5½ miles between Glasgow and Renfrew, twelve shoals, one having only 15 inches at low water, and four only 18 inches each, but carrying out an act obtained in 1770, authorising the deepening of the channel to at least 7 feet in low water, one John Golborne of Chester got a contract in 1772 from the Municipality to deepen the Dumbuck Ford to at least

QUEEN'S DOCK, GLASGOW (S. BASIN)

6 feet, and actually accomplished a depth of 7 feet, which was increased in a few years to 14 feet through the increased scour of the river produced by the contraction of the stream by means of rubble jetties. The sand and silt of flood and tide filled up the space between the jetties and made excellent reclaimed land for which the future Clyde Trust had to pay right handsomely to the riparian proprietors when subsequent widening of the river was demanded.

Golborne's improvements gave Glasgow for the first time the status of a real port, though they cost a sum which must have seemed alarming to the municipality of the time, when the revenue of the river was less than £10 per annum. It was on the theory that navigable channels of tidal rivers depend on tidal ebb and flow, and not upon the natural stream or floods, that Golborne operated, and he acted on the principle of increasing the tidal volume and prolonging its flow upwards by dredging, and by filling up indents which tended to create eddies, a principle followed by his successor Rennie, who further contracted the bounds of the river by connecting Golborne's jetties by dykes running parallel with the stream. Little more than a hundred years ago high-water was hardly perceptible at Glasgow, it came up in an insignificant ripple; now there is an 11 feet range of tide, and a good deal of the depth has been obtained, not by the raising of the high-water mark, but by dredging out the bottom of the channel, which is now virtually level from the Broomielaw to Port Glasgow. The tide—such as it was—at Glasgow a hundred years ago was three hours later than at Port Glasgow; it is now only one hour later. These are circumstances that eloquently prove the soundness of Golborne's engineering principle.

But the greatest enterprises of the river authorities originated after 1840, when the management of river affairs passed out of the hands of the Magistrates and Town Council and was transferred to a separate board called the Clyde Navigation Trust, of which the majority were Town Councillors and others represented outside bodies like the Chamber of Commerce, the Merchants' House, the Trades' House, and two or three neighbouring burghs. It has sometimes been questioned in later years if the amenities of the river sides at Glasgow would not have been more carefully preserved by the continued maintenance of an elected body responsible to the ratepayers for all they did, but the commercial enterprise and foresight of the Trust are indisputable, and whatever the general ratepayers of Glasgow may think now, they appear complacently prepared to trust implicitly to a body which naturally places the interests of ship-owners and shippers before all others. In 1840 an Act was passed authorising the deepening of the harbour and river throughout to at least 17 feet at neap tides, and laying down lines for future widening. The greatest natural obstacle proved to be a rock at Elderslie discovered by the grounding of a ship in 1854, and extending across the river and for nearly 1000 feet of its length. It cost £70,000 to cut through this trap reef to a depth of

20 feet below low water, and its final removal has only recently been accomplished.

Meanwhile the whole character of marine traffic was undergoing a revolution. In 1847 sailing ships were the only deep sea traders, and their loading and discharging berths for cargo not dealt with at the Tail of the Bank lay between Oswald Street and James Watt Street. Glasgow was still, as a port, subsidiary to Greenock, whence many trans-shipped cargoes had to be taken by lighter, and Glasgow merchants sorely grudged the heavy tolls which Greenock levied on all cargo passing to the City. The necessity for deepening the river and straightening its channel was constantly pressed upon the Trustees, who were timid and inclined to dole out the needed funds with a niggard hand. The marine engine, whose coming had made more obvious the shortcomings of the river in respect of draught, also brought the cure—for the steam hopper barge was put to dredge the channel, and has been doing so ever since with results more quickly apparent than under the old system, where ploughs, hauled by horses or capstans, worked under the banks at low water, or a tug boat leisurely dragged a harrow over the bottom. In 1863 vessels with draughts ranging from 14 feet to 21 feet frequently grounded in the river; taking several tides, and sometimes having to be partially unladen to get up and down. To-day vessels of 27 feet draught freely traverse the river, one drawing 28 feet lately accomplished the trip in a single tide, and widening and straightening of the channel have kept pace with deepening, to the immense improvement of navigation. At that date the harbour east of the Kelvin, which was its western limit, had an area of only seventy acres of water space, and famous shipbuilding yards—Napiers, Thomsons, the early Barclay Curles', Stephens, and Connells—were still situated within the harbour limits. The sites of these yards were purchased by the Clyde Trustees, and converted into docks and quays, the shipbuilding industry moving further down the river. The first dock—the Kingston, opened on the south side of the river in 1867—was a small basin of five acres on the site of a sand-pit with 830 lineal yards of quays. Ten years later the Queen's Dock at Stobcross took in ships where previously had been a farm and market garden, and has now a water area of 34 acres, with 3300 lineal yards of quayage. The Prince's Dock on the south side, opened by the Duke of York in 1897, was also a market garden, and is somewhat larger than the Queen's; and the latest of the Docks, the Rothesay, with electrical appliances for loading and discharging mineral—its main purpose—is of its kind unsurpassed in any part of the country.

Up till 1875 there was no graving dock on the upper Clyde, though Tod & M'Gregor had one on the Kelvin, and large steamers requiring repairs had to go to Greenock or Liverpool. The Clyde Trust has now three suited for the largest steamers, and other private docks exist. It has five-and-a-third miles of sheds and a floor area in them of nearly forty-seven acres, eight times more than in 1863; it has ninety-five cranes, lifting from 130 tons downwards, all worked either by steam, hydraulic or electrical power; at Yorkhill, Meadowside, and Merklands, and on the lands of Shieldhall, Shiels and Braehead down to Renfrew it has provided on a huge scale by purchases of land for the extension of quays and docks in the future; all its docks are connected by rail to the various trunk lines, and there are 22 miles of harbour tramways. Only in recent years did an excellent system of small passenger steamers, established to ferry up and down the river, succumb to the competition of the Glasgow Corporation Tramcars along the river lines, but its cross-river ferries carry ten millions of passengers and half a million of vehicles per annum. Since the transfer of the undertaking from the municipality to the Clyde Trust, the financing of the Trust's operations has been all its own credit without any Government or Municipal aid whatsoever, and the confidence of the investing public is evident from the ease with which capital can be raised. In 1863 the Trust had spent on the undertaking, apart from the cost of maintenance, which was charged to revenue, £1,465,852. Since then a further sum of £6,929,444 had been outlaid, making a total capital outlay of £8,395,296. But the resources derived from the dues levied on the trade of the port had been such that the debt of the Trust was only £6,338,016. Their property thus stood at more than two millions less than its cost. The revenue in 1863 was £118,083; in 1906 it was £528,569—nearly four and a half times more. But the increase was derived in many instances from a lower and deliberately reduced scale of dues as regarded goods, to which it alone applied for the encouragement of trade. The Trust is not carried on for profit. Its business is to make provision for the existing trade of the port and for its probable expansion, and, having made that provision, to distribute its annual cost judiciously and equitably over the commerce it brings, keeping always in hand a portion of the revenue—a surplus for contingencies. As to the ships and goods which provided the revenue, there were of ships in 1863, 15,175 arrivals and a like number of departures, making the taxed number 30,350, of an aggregate inward and outward net tonnage of 3,055,558 tons. In 1906 the numbers in and out were 31,927—not a great numerical increase; but their aggregate net tonnage in and out was 11,022,183 tons—more than three and a half times greater. Of goods, in 1863 in and out there were 1,437,235 tons. In 1906 in and out there were 9,035,028 tons.

OLD KILPATRICK, LOOKING WEST

CHAPTER X

HARBOUR LIFE

LIKE Melrose, Glasgow Harbour should perhaps be seen at night, or at the end of an Autumn afternoon, when a swollen sun, setting behind thickets of masts, gilding the stream, glorifying smoky cloud, transfiguring dingy store and tenement, closes a vista that captivates the eye and spurs the imagination as might some vision of a Venice stained and fallen from virtue, an abandoned mistress of the sea. In such an hour and season we forget the cost of mercantile supremacy, and see in that wide fissure through the close-packed town a golden pathway to romance, or the highway home to our native hills and isles. The other aspect—that of dark bewildering hours, is only known most poignantly to native sailors who carry about the world with them a not unpleasing thought of a familiar Avernus full of phantom fleets whereof one special ship must be discovered ere the dawn; an Avernus intricate, and ill to traverse, with a head bemused by farewell rum; with dancing lights on the foul high tide, roaring Lucigen flares, sheds gulping a ghostly radiance; with sounds of chains, cranes, capstans; the panting of sleepless engines, the cries of spectre stevedores and lumpers; with odours of spice and tar, wine, fruit, oil, hides, and a thousand other pungent sweet or acrid things unknown. The ship (with luck) is found, her Blue Peter high at the truck, though unseen in the darkness; the Old Man swears at the lubberly late-comer, who awkwardly bears his dunnage over the gang-plank; friends on the quay edge cry after him, "Ye didna shake hands, Jack," to which he retorts: "Lord! neither I did; ach! it doesna maitter; I'll be back in a year or twa." And so, carelessly, goes forth to the mercy of sea and storm another fearless spirit with a vast deal more of sentiment in his soul than you might think to hear that last good-bye.

Come to the harbours by day, and then I grant there is little glamour to be found; come on a wet November day especially, to look for some not particularly distinguishable shipping-box at the far end of some not very distinctive mile-long quay, and before you have found it the melancholy of things will have bitten to your very heart. I do not wonder that to all but those whose business takes them there, the harbour, whose name is known to the uttermost ends of the earth, should be wholly unfamiliar to Glasgow citizens. They may see the upper end of it from the train as they cross on the railway bridges morning and afternoon from and to suburban villas or the coast; they may once or twice have ventured down the channel in a "Clutha," to feel some vague emotion in a scene so strange, but as a rule the harbour, with its vast activities, its "earnest of romance," lies wholly beyond their interest or curiosity. They would as soon think of going to St. Joceline's Crypt. Streets noisy and unbeautiful lead down to it from either side; its waters do not invite to acquatic recreation. Itinerant bagpipers (invariably playing "The Cock o' the North") discourage the sensitive intruder from the most feasible entrance to it at the side of the Jamaica Bridge, and all the other less obvious portals are apt to be encumbered by an intoxicated mercantile marine, or by mighty waggons laden with boiler plates that traverse the granite setts with a din infernal.

It is a pity the up-and-down river service of little "Clutha" steamers is no more, for if it was not profitable to the coffers of the Clyde Trustees who owned the vessels, it kept the city in touch with what has really made its fortunes and made more manifest the Trust's importance. Yet it is still possible to pass the harbour in review by going on one of the many steamers that daily sail from the Broomielaw for the towns upon the Firth. The Broomielaw is really Glasgow's heart, though some folk think it is George Square. The name to-day seems quite ironic, for neither Broom nor Law is obvious there, where Glasgow Bridge divides the harbour proper from the upper stream that flows by less busy, more neglected banks past the Green; but once the yellow flowers of *planta genista* flourished there, when our grandfathers could ford the river with their kilts tucked up. There is here no spacious channel like the Mersey, but only a fairway of 620 feet at its widest and 362 at its narrowest point; nor closely hemming warehouses such as on the Thames appear to court disaster for their windows from the yards of ships. The clean, gay, holiday-looking steamers for the coast seem half intruders, and out of harmony with the squat long lines of cargo sheds, and the piles of offices and dwelling-houses in their rear; you can fancy that they gladly steam away each morning to a "cleaner, greener land." Going with them you pass wharves lined at first by packets that ply to English and Irish ports; then by berths where greatly favoured big Atlantic, Mediterranean and Indian liners —Allan and Anchor—safely warp among countless hazards from puffing tugs and unwieldy hopper dredgers; then by the jaws of docks, and past ferries, and into the far-extending region where the shipbuilding yards have gathered, and so on to the meadows, and finally to the welcome sea.

There are innumerable tales of what the passenger has said on such a harbour voyage, and how the captain —witty fellow!—made reply; they are in all the other books about the Clyde, and need not be repeated. The raconteur, in truth, is an impertinent intrusion on the sentiment of this Titanic scene, wherein etcher and painter have discovered aspects arresting and sublime, for all the dullness and even ugliness of the details. More patently obtrusive to the voyagers I must confess will seem the odour of which the cleansing operations of the city have not yet wholly rid the oily water we traverse. If the city fathers, however, have been slow to find conviction of the sin it is to pollute their river, they have entered on the process of regeneration in no niggard spirit, and the result of their great new sewage operations is apparent already. A pleasing tag for municipal banquet speeches and for the humorists of the local press has reference to the imminent restoration of the salmon at the Broomielaw. We can scarcely hope for angling at Stobcross or Pointhouse Ferry, Highland Lane or Linthouse, but even now, bewildered trout and surely foolish grilse, inheriting some instinct for the linns where their forebears spawned among the hills, are found curiously forcing their way through the wake of steamers in the harbour or struggling in the basins, to be captured and stuffed for some riverside parlour and furnish forth another airy paragraph.

And yet it is not on a steamer one can get at the veritable heart of the harbour; for that takes days and nights and seasons. One must haunt the ferries, whose low-hulled craft traverse the stream incessantly, bearing the workers to and from their toil; one must linger on the quays and listen to the jabber of Gaelic and Irish "hands," pilots, and ferrymen; of Lascars shivering in thin dongarees, bent—poor misguided souls!—on imposing shells upon a "sea-born" city; of Spanish onion-sellers, fezzed Greeks with sample rugs and gold embroidery; truculent Dago rogues with ugly knives; Dutch nondescripts looking askance at frowzy women from the slums, sometimes a slit-eyed Chinese, or Barbadian—"true Badian born, neither crab nor Creole" ; furtive native crimps, silk-capped coal-trimmers, fussy super-cargoes, brass-bound mates, German, Galician, Doukhabor, and Scandinavian emigrants. One must see the ships disgorge themselves under mighty derricks, of ore from New Caledonia, timber from Oregon, nitrates from Iquique ; crates of odorous fruit from Spain, tuns of wine from France and Portugal ; palm oil and ivory from South Africa, cotton, tea, spice, and jute from India ; tea from China ; cattle, corn, flour, beef, scantlings, and doors and windows ready-made from the United States ; wheat from Canada, Egypt and Russia ; sugar, teak and mahogany from the West Indies, tinned food and gold from Australasia.

Nor even then can one rightly comprehend the harbour who has not brooded beside sheer-leg and crane-jib that are mightily moving enormous weights as if they had been toys ; swallowed the coal-dust of the docks, dodged traction engines, eaten Irish stew for breakfast in the Sailors' Home, watched Geordie Geddes trawl for corpses, sat in the fo'c'sles of "tramps," stood in a fog by the pilot on the bridge, heard the sorrows of a Shore Superintendent and the loyal lies of witnesses in a Board of Trade examination, who feel bound to "stick by the owners" and swear their engines backed ten minutes before the accident ; or sat on a cask in the Prince's Dock on peaceful Sabbath mornings when the shipping seemed asleep, or an unseen concertina played some sailor's jig for canticle.

As for the types of vessels you shall meet there, I

BOWLING, IRISH BARQUES UNLOADING KELP

cannot do better than quote from the talented authors of "Glasgow in 1901," who deal with our harbour lovingly. "The liner de luxe, as Liverpool people understand her in the *Oceanic* or the *Campania* or the *St. Louis*, is not to be seen on the narrow Clyde, and the Cardiff man, accustomed to his miles of coal traders, will find disappointment here; still, if you were to spend a diligent morning in the docks, you will find few types of the British mercantile marine amissing. The Transatlantic passenger steamers of the Allan and Anchor firms; the strange East-Coastish lines of the Donaldson carriers ('lines like a hat-box,' as an old shipper had it), the queer shaped turret ships of the Clan Company, which look as though they had swallowed more cargo than they could digest, the big bright-funnelled South American traders, bristling with derricks and samson-posts; the China Mutual steamers, with their names in the script of Far Cathay on their bows; the Loch Line sailing ships, which clip Australian records every season as keen as any 'grey-hound of the Atlantic'; the four-masted Frenchmen from New Caledonia, the teak-carrier from Rangoon, the auxiliary screw laden with seal oil and skins from Harbour Grace, the nitrite barque from Chili, the City steamers from India and the Persian Gulf—you can find them all. Then there are the squadrons of tramps that thrash from Bilbao to the Clyde with ore and back again with coal; the Italian fruit boats, the stout cross-channel packets, the Highland steamers, and top-sail schooners which congregate in the Kingston Dock."

The Harbour life slops over its actual precincts, and the neighbouring streets, as in other ports, bear a marine impress. Their tall "lands" of flats fed from a common stair are the homes of folk whose men are "on the quays" or "sailing foreign" or "stoking on the old *Furnessia*"; there is no seaman so black or poor that he cannot get some kind of a lodging there. Ship-chandlers' shops, slop shops, shops where binnacle lights, patent logs, and sextants, marlin and Nautical Almanacks fill the windows, others that delight the eye of youth with visions of sheath-knives and revolvers, and the coin and paper currency of every imaginable foreign State, are there, and licensed shops innumerable that seek the suffrages of the sailorman by making a speciality of the "schooner" of beer at twopence. High over all is the tower of the Sailors' Home at the Broomielaw, now-a-days a good deal too far east of the busy docks for Jack's convenience.

CHAPTER XI

THE SHIP-SHOP

If the native of Glasgow, travelling abroad and advertising himself vaingloriously as of the "Second City in the Kingdom," is often vexed to find it adds nothing to his importance, he is almost always sure of some solace to his wounded pride when he goes on steamers. He finds so often there, above some flashing mass of enginery, or on a not too unobtrusive panel, a brazen legend that informs him what he looks upon was made upon the Clyde. I have known a Glasgow child, in the streets of Cairo, gaze transported on a boiler, which, carted through Eastern traffic, seemed the embodiment of ugliness or incongruity, but had for her a charm because it showed, white-painted on its ends, the name of "Polmadie." "I should like to hug that old boiler!" she exclaimed, and it is perhaps in search of some such happy pang of home association that Glasgow men, steam-sailing anywhere, are so prone to go below to "see the engines." They really want to be assured that all is well with the workmanship of the crafts to which they trust their precious lives.

> "Glasgow ships come sailing in, come sailing in,
> Come sailing in,"

says our old school-time rhyme, and indeed Glasgow ships come sailing into every open harbour in the world. They are found in the oddest waters; they have been taken by the Kara Sea and the Yenisei River to Lake Baikal in the heart of Asia; in parts, like nursery picture-blocks, they have been put together on the inland seas of North America. There are twin-screw awning deckers on the Amazon, Khedival yachts on the Red Sea, stern-wheelers in South African rivers, Rajahs' paddle-galleys on the shores of Sarawak, and nondescripts for gospel purposes or for worldly trade in the lakes of Central Africa, which came to life under our smoky northern sky, beneath the hands of Glasgow rivet-boys. Clyde clippers have broken records and held them long in the days of the "wind-jammer," when each trip from China or Australia was a feverish race, and Clyde steamers, since the marine engine came to being, have had a *cachet* like Sheffield cutlery or the buns of Bath, so that the praise of them is a convention of English literature, and Kipling and Conrad, voicing the sentiment of the seaman, credit their heroic ships, their shrewdest engineers, to Clyde; our very dredgers keep innumerable ports and rivers navigable in countries where the name of Glasgow, or Simons &

Co. is unpronounceable. So much for the ships of peace; Clyde-built men of war, like the old Scots soldiers of fortune, have fought under strange flags, and there has probably been no sea-fight in the last half-century, in which a grimy Scottish engineer could not be found deep in the hot heart of some furious combatant, careless, maybe, of the cause his vessel fought for, but cherishing his beloved engines, which knew only his language, best understood his touch, ministering most willingly to him because he came from the place of their conception. Strange men, foreign-looking, anti-Christian to our suspicious Presbyterian eyes, though maybe to be found with human qualities under the ameliorative influence of the senior partner's bottle, come from all the sea-beat borders of the world to buy Clyde boats, as women go to market, certain of finding all they want so long as they have the money to pay for it. To-day it is a Californian owner—half Scot, half Irish, now of Nob Hill, but once of Paradise, Port Glasgow—who wants, in ten months, a 5000 ton cargo steamer for the Pacific. He will register her, when he gets her, as of Glasgow, and take her home tariff free, to change her port of registry to Vancouver as soon as may be convenient. To-morrow it will be a sun-bronzed, crisp-haired, Spanish-spoken gentleman with an order in his pocket for a cruiser for Peru or San Domingo. Again, it is a stranger seeking "tramps," and the provision of cargo-carriers classed under that eloquent appellation is so easy a task to the lower

Clyde, and carried out so expeditiously, that the builders are said to construct hulls by the mile, and saw them up in the requisite lengths to order with a dent at the ends to finish them. The dent is always water-tight. It would be a marvellous taste in vessels that could not be accommodated in this ship-shop; its keepers have plans and models (the latter made at incredible cost by artists of the miniature) comprising every new development, anticipating the requirements of to-morrow; even if freaks be your foible they will make you them—Fairfield built the *Livadia*, weirdest of marine monsters, for the Czar. You may find sometimes that the very ship you want is ready waiting for you, since the builders, knowing the world must move, knowing what it ought to have, and certain it must have it sooner or later, build ships "on spec" in slack seasons, and so keep their men employed.

So much for ships at first hand; Clyde ships, second-hand, grown obsolete for Glasgow passengers, go, at the end, to less fastidious quarters, so that "crocks" from the Clyde have glorified the lower Thames and provided a standard of elegance for the traveller to Clacton and Southend; and elsewhere in English waters the Scotsman often comes upon old friends of the "Fair" holidays working under aliases. Such good stuff are those old Clyde passenger steamers that they seem immortal, and their owners buff out the natal dates on their bells and engine brasses, ashamed, perhaps, to be found demanding the labour of youth from such veterans.

ENTRANCE TO CLYDE AND FORTH CANAL,
BOWLING

The Ship-Shop

For two reasons the Clyde can claim to be the greatest of shipbuilding centres in a shipbuilding age. She is the mother-lodge in the freemasonry of men who build fleets, whether it be on Thames, Belfast or Stettin, for the first passenger steamboat in Britain was launched upon her waters and almost all the great discoveries in marine engineering were made or tested first upon her banks. If Stettin and Belfast, having borrowed her brains for a while in recent years, have challenged her supremacy in the production of ocean liners that should be bigger and faster than all others, she has again, by the advent of the *Lusitania* recovered such prestige as lies in tonnage and speed. "When you want apples," said Yarrow of Poplar, "you go to Covent Garden; for meat to a meat market, and for ships you go to the North." The four chief reasons are that here we have cheap coal, cheap iron, cheaper labour, and cheaper rates, so men like Yarrow leave the Thames and establish themselves in the Scottish ship-shop.

I have said the first passenger steamboat ever built in Britain was launched upon the Clyde; it was the forty-two feet *Comet* of 1812, with a three horse power engine, working at a pressure of five pounds to the square inch, built in Port-Glasgow for Henry Bell, an enterprising inn-keeper of Helensburgh, whereto she sailed deliberately three times a week from the Broomielaw. The sloop-sailors of the time, looking at her puffing seaward, fervently thanked God they went by "the Almichty's ain win' and no' wi' the deevil's sunfire and brimstane." The story of the

Clyde since then is the story of the steamer. Having proved the practicability of propelling ships by steam-driven paddles, local genius sought at once, with Scottish thrift, to do it economically. Men rose then who seemed to give themselves as with poetic ecstasy to the revelation of the power of this new agent in the destiny of man—the Napiers, the Dennys, and the Cairds; John Elder, John Wood, William Pearce; the Thomsons, Tod & M'Gregor, Russells, Stephens, Connells, Scotts, Hendersons, Rodgers, Barclay Curles, Simons, and Inglis. By the earliest of them were invented and applied the surface condenser and the compound, triple, and quadruple engine: the screw propeller for ocean steaming, and the change of hull material from wood to iron and from iron to steel if elsewhere first suggested, were developments which for years were in the hands of Clydeside men. A Partick firm no longer in existence, Tod & M'Gregor, inaugurated the age of the deep sea iron steamer sixty years ago, and Wingate of Whiteinch made the engines of the *Sirius*, the first vessel to cross the Atlantic under steam, and virtually reduce the breadth of that waterway by one-half, to the great gain of the sufferer from *mal-de-mer*. From 1840 to 1899 (with coquettish intervals of no great duration, during which they went elsewhere) the great ship companies remained constant to the Clyde, and here by Napier were built the first Cunarders —wooden paddle ships of about 1100 tons; midgets compared with the *Lusitania*; the first of the Inman Liners and the Royal Mail Steam Packets; the pick of the Orient line, the Castle, Union, Pacific, British India, P. & O., Allan, Anchor, Canadian Pacific. Continental fleets of merchantmen came for long from the same river; the Norddeutscher-Lloyd started with seven Fairfield ships; Caird alone has built a score of Hamburg American packets, and second-hand Clyde liners pioneered the enterprise of the Compagnie Generale Transatlantique.

To-day, nearly all the high-speed cross-channel services are maintained by Clyde-built vessels, and the summer fleets of the Thames, the Solent, Bristol Channel, and Belfast Lough have, at their best, the same origin, as of course have also the swift luxurious passenger boats of our own estuary. As a centre of yacht designing and yacht building the Clyde has no serious rival in the world; the fame of G. L. Watson and the Fifes of Fairlie rests upon racers and steam yachts here constructed; *Shamrocks* grown on our banks persistently struggle for an elusive America Cup, and American millionaires come here for the floating pleasure palaces of which Gordon Bennett's *Lysistrata* and Drexel's *Marguerita* may be looked upon as the "top notch" in luxury. These for peace; for war the Clyde has provided the British Admiralty with almost every class of fighting ship, and contributed to the navies of nearly every maritime state in the world.

It may well astound the stranger, passing for the first time down the narrow ribbon of murky water between the clamorous yards, that any ship at all should find her way from the stocks to the safe entrance of what we call her "native element." In other quarters hulls are sometimes built broadside to rivers, and so in due time slide to life: here they grow at an angle on keel-block and cradle, and at the release of triggers, a mammoth like the *Lusitania* slides down the well greased ways to float in 86 seconds, yet with a velocity so moderate that she is brought up to her 1000 ton drags with her bow about 110 feet from the shore.

CHAPTER XII

THE LOWER REACHES

GLASGOW, with a gust, as it were, for the sea-breeze and the evening sun, has always stretched her arms importunate to the west. A day may come when she shall climb to the wholesome breezy plateau of the Mearns to the south of her; indeed her tram-cars are almost there already reconnoitring; but for long she has, by preference keeping close to the river banks, crept seaward, usurping towns and hamlets on the way, and it looks as if she will not be content until she dips her feet in the waves that beat against Dumbarton rock. Govan and Partick, far west of old St. Mungo's bounds, have in a sense already gone the way of Anderston and Finnieston, though municipally they refuse to acknowledge it; they have been swallowed up by their great neighbour—octopus they unkindly term her—and though they exist as independent burghs they are, to the eye, actual parts of Glasgow, incorporated so closely in the westward rush of streets that they have even ceased to be suburban in almost any aspect. It is not without its pathos, this submergence of old isolate small communities in the torrent of a great town's progress, and we can surely spare a little sympathy for those that resist though their ultimate capitulation is only a question of time.

Govan, but for the possession of a Provost of its own, and a different design in lamp-posts, is virtually as much a part of Glasgow as Bermondsey is of London; there is no breach in the continuity of noisy, high-walled and thickly populated streets that lead to it from the city's heart; nothing survives of the rural character it had in the 1830's when the gourmets of Glasgow—with cautious circumlocution for fear of the elders, you may be sure—used to walk there for its famous Sunday salmon suppers which gave it a local fame as great as Greenwich has earned by its white-bait. Except for the reckless and ill-fated fish I have already referred to as venturing at long intervals up to the docks, the only salmon to come to Govan nowadays arrives in cans from British Columbia, but there are men alive who recollect the fishery which existed here long after nets were drawn for the last time on green banks where now are the wharves of Glasgow.

Doubtless its pleasant situation opposite the confluence of the Kelvin gave it favour in the sight of the ever-judicious and decerning early ecclesiastics, who built a cell or church here, and later a monastery. Its windows looked to the west, on tidal marshes noisy with sea-fowl, broken by reedy

HENRY BELL'S MONUMENT AND
DUNGLASS CASTLE

isles and promontories. The lands were granted to the church in 1152, about which time Bishop Herbert erected the church of Govan into a prebend of the Glasgow Cathedral, with an endowment of islands *ex adverso*, that are no longer in existence. For centuries the pulpit of Govan was supplied by ministers elected by the Glasgow University authorities, the most notable of them, Andrew Melville, Principal of Glasgow and St. Andrews, who took the liberty of remonstrating with the Lord's Anointed James the Sixth, and ridiculing a service in the Chapel Royal in a Latin epigram, found himself in consequence a prisoner for four years in the Tower of London. Poor man! he must have missed his caller salmon! Otherwise Govan figures modestly in history. What fame it enjoys is modern and devoid of any associations to stay the foot of poet, artist, or sentimentalist. Its prosperity has been wholly due to the necessity for new shipyards when the old ones impeding the Glasgow harbour had to be abandoned, and in ten years—1871 to 1881—its population rose from 19,000 to 52,000. To-day it is the fifth burgh in Scotland, royal, parliamentary, or otherwise, with a population of over 82,000 in the census of 1901, and its parish—which embraces many of the districts and smaller burghs on both sides of the Clyde—is one of the richest in Scotland, as may be guessed from the imposing nature of its kirk.

Fairfield Shipbuilding Yard has given Govan a world-wide reputation for the construction of ships, and the story of Fairfield's rise is what journalism with cheerful recklessness of the meaning of words has often called "one of the romances of modern industry." In 1834 Mr. Charles Randolph and Mr. R. S. Cunliff started a small wheel-wright's business under the "style" of Randolph & Co.; their pay-roll for the first year aggregated a little over £1000, and their turnover less than three times that figure. Till 1852 shipbuilding was no part of the firm's enterprise, but in that year it was joined by one John Elder, a Glasgow man, whose share in the development of the steam-engine is second only to that of James Watt, and the firm of Randolph, Elder & Co. became in time the biggest shipbuilding concern in the world. In 1860 the firm began ship-building above Govan Ferry; in 1864 the present yard at Fairfield was opened, and in five months four ships were built to run the American blockade. Elder died in 1869 at the early age of 45, and a statue stands to his memory in the public park presented to the people of Govan by his widow. There were certain mutations in the firm thereafter, but under William Pearce, a man of Kent, who became its sole proprietor in 1878, and the Limited Liability Company which succeeded him and still maintains the business, Fairfield has vastly added to its resources and reputation.

On the opposite side of the river and on the west bank of the tributary Kelvin, is the burgh of Partick. "The midnight fairies" of Tom Lyle's song convene

no more in Kelvingrove, though the nurse-maid and her "lad" may tryst by the weirs in the park below Gilmorehill; he would be an extravagant idealist who would invite his lover now to

"wander by the mill, bonnie lassie, O,
To the cove beside the rill, bonnie lassie, O,
Where the glens rebound the call
Of the roaring water's fall,
Through the mountain's rocky hall, bonnie lassie, O."

The Kelvin, in truth, loses all its idyllic aspects before it comes to Partick, and ends its career unpleasantly in the slip and graving-docks of Pointhouse and Meadowside. Partick or "Perdeyc" was at one time held by the Archbishop of Glasgow for payment of a silver merk per annum, and was bestowed by King David upon the church of St. Kentigern in 1136, on the occasion of the dedication of the newly built Cathedral. A century later it was an episcopal residence. At the close of last century, Partick, where the gourmets who patronised the salmon suppers of Govan came alternately to the "bun and yill house" for (*inter alia*) "crumpie cakes and cheese," was a little hamlet which Dr. Strang the historian of the Glasgow clubs fondly describes as "nestling among umbrageous trees, and standing by the side of a limpid and gurgling stream which flowed through its centre." Life itself flowed like that in Partick then, to the sleepy clack of flour mills. The most notable of the mills, on whose site now stands a massive modern flour factory, was a tribute to that much misdoubted thing, the gratitude of princes, for the land on which it stood was granted to the Incorporation of Glasgow Bakers in 1568 by the Regent Murray, in recognition of the highly satisfactory manner in which they had supplied his troops with the "baps" on the strength of which they won the Battle of Langside. 'Tis strange to think that stourey Glasgow bakers had some share in the shame of that dreadful scene at Fotheringay! Partick to-day almost shares with Hillhead the glory of being Glasgow's West End, but the ultra fashionable, who frequent the West of Scotland Cricket Ground in the season, aspire to call themselves of Partickhill or Dowanhill, since the name of the burgh much too obviously suggests a social clamjamfry.

Whiteinch, Yoker, Clydebank, Kilbowie and Dalmuir, all on the north side of the Clyde between the Kelvin and the Kilpatrick hills, are towns whose origin is of yesterday; they are the homes of men who work in the shipyards or in the huge factory of the Singer Sewing Machine Company whose clock tower dominates the smoky valley. Thirty years ago the district now covered with "lands" of houses, vast blocks of workshops, chimney stacks and lines of railway, was purely pastoral, and it must have been from a view of it that John Burroughs, aforesaid, describing his passage by ship up the river, said she "steered her way amid turnip fields and broad acres of newly planted potatoes." With the towns named we have no pastoral associations now; their mention brings to the mind but thoughts of shrieking and insistent sirens heralding wet winter morns, the clatter of toilward feet on muddy pavements, a manner of life strenuous and unlovely. The Clydebank shipbuilding yard—once G. and J. Thomson's, famous all over the world as birthplace of notable Cunarders, P. and O., Union, and Inman liners, and more recently known as John Brown and Co.'s—has in the present year produced the *Lusitania*; it faces the river Cart; beside it is the latest of Glasgow's docks—the Rothesay, formally opened in April, 1907, by the Prince and Princess of Wales.

To come to the Cart was at one time to be tempted up to Paisley, the town of bards and bobbins on its banks, three miles from its junction with the Clyde, but the Cart (with a small shipbuilding reputation of its own) could inspire poets like Burns, Campbell and Tannahill only in its upper reaches, and Paisley—Vanduara of the ancient Ptolemy, possessed of a fine old abbey and the greatest thread-spinning works in the world—is beyond the limits of our survey. Elderslie, the birthplace of William Wallace, lies 2½ miles to the west of it in a country fertile and interesting. But before we come to Cart, thirty minutes' sail or so from Glasgow is the town of Renfrew, one of the oldest burghs in Scotland, which has the honour of giving a title to the Prince of Wales. Renfrew is on the south bank of the river at the mouth of a burn which has never lived down the saddening fact that it is called the Pudzeoch. On Blaeu's old maps the town is shown to have been on the very margin of a loop of the Clyde which surrounded an island at this point, and the yards of boats in Renfrew harbour sometimes broke the windows of the manse; but the island is no more, and Renfrew proper is half a mile from the river now—a town of one long street and numerous lanes and wynds that branch off irregularly from it. Doubtless it has statistics, but I recall more easily its bohemian suppers; a "Tattie and Herring Incorporation" having for over a hundred years brought to its inn the kind of Paisley "buddy" and Glasgow man who can combine some soul of melody and mirth with that simple fare. To be in close proximity to old manorial families has in many instances restrained the development of many communities in the West of Scotland: and Renfrew to the west is bounded by the "policies" of Lord Blythswood. Paisley, with its more obvious claims to the ministrations of the railway, might, in any case, have diverted traffic and trade away from the banks of Clyde at this point and left Renfrew what it is—a dull terminus at the end of an unimportant branch line, with the most eloquent name in the world for dredgers—the specialty of Simons & Co., and for Babcock & Wilcox water-tube boilers,—but it is possible too that the beautiful old acres of Blythswood, and of Lord Blantyre at Erskine, had special consideration from the men who have elsewhere ruthlessly broken up ancient landmarks. In any case Renfrew has in recent generations been preserved from total extinction

THE MARSHES BELOW BOWLING

only by the presence of the shipbuilding yards in its neighbourhood. It was a place of some importance as early as the twelfth century, and has been a Royal Burgh since 1396. In the beginning of the seventeenth century it was the principal port on the Clyde, whose trustees still pay an annual indemnity to it for spoiling its salmon fishing privileges.

If the jealous preservation of Blythswood House and its pastoral amenities may find no favour from the hardened economist who counts each great new town an unquestionable gain for human happiness, there are people otherwise minded who will rejoice that the encroaching city has so long been held in check on the south side of the river by such pleasant interludes of nature. Blythswood House is not old, and the name itself has only in recent times been borrowed from a small but now precious part of Glasgow surrounding Blythswood Square, belonging to the Campbell of Blythswood family. A stone in the grounds marks the spot where Archibald Campbell, ninth Earl of Argyll, was captured in the disguise of a peasant in 1685. The estate, like that of Erskine on the same side further down the river—Inchinnan intervening—is perhaps a little too flat for a taste nurtured in the rugged north, but the beauty of the suave parks and graceful woods in both instances is undeniable. Up till the middle of the nineteenth century, Erskine was the ancient patrimony of the Earls of Mar, who took their family name from it. Passing through the hands of the Hamiltons of

Orbiston, it was purchased in 1703 by Lord Blantyre, and still belongs to that family. The Tudoresque mansion now to be seen on a rise of ground back from the river was built in 1828 from designs by Sir Robert Smirke. It looks over the widening river to the shire of Dumbarton and the hills of Kilpatrick.

CHAPTER XIII

LENNOX

At Erskine Ferry, where the river in certain aspects recalled the Kentish Thames to Dorothy Wordsworth, if to nobody else, we are really at the portals of the Firth, and the hills on the north side of the river, furrowed by hurried streams and scarred by storm, are the *avant-gardes* of the veritable Highlands. Old Kilpatrick lies at the foot of them—a tranquil little town identified by tradition with the nativity of St. Patrick, patron saint of Ireland. This claim for Kilpatrick is, I regret to say, contested by some foolish place called Boulogne-sur-mer, but locally we laugh at that. No one, at least, can wrest from Kilpatrick the glory of having in the confines of its parish had the western terminal forts of that thirty-six-and-a-half-mile turfen wall which Antoninus, by his legate Lollius Urbicus, built between the Forth and Clyde. Nature had defrayed the first expense of the redoubts, and Chapel Hill, an eminence beside the village, has rewarded the assiduity of antiquarian search by *trouvailles* of Roman monumental tablets, vases, and coins, that are now preserved in the Hunterian Museum of Glasgow, "which is somewhat similar to being reinterred," as Hugh Macdonald puts it.

From the foot-hills of Kilpatrick the alien keepers of the *vallum* had a noble view, which has lost none of its charm in a thousand years, unless we count the smoke-stacks of the ships in Bowling harbour a poor equivalent for the long sweeps and beaked prows of the Roman galleys which sheltered in the lee of Dumbarton or under the Hill of Dun. No finer panorama of the Clyde may elsewhere be discovered; Sam Bough has made the most of it in one memorable canvas; Horatio M'Culloch was never more happily inspired than in "Dalnottar Hill"; Nasmyth painted in the neighbourhood a drop scene which, for old habitues of the Glasgow Queen Street Theatre, was as exhilarating as a day "doon the water."

Yet Old Kilpatrick is no way maritime: fields and the railway separate it from the river shore, on which there is a shipbuilding yard, and Bowling is the port. Bowling—now the hailing station of the Glasgow harbour-master—is at the western extremity of the Forth and Clyde Canal, and in its basin the best of the passenger steamers on the coast are wintered, to have the rust-scale tapped from their hulls and their toilets made for the following spring. It is always in terms of comedy that the West refers to Bowling, since the life which is inspired by a canal has ever seemed in a way contemptible to men who pass it in great ships from the great seas, yet the village, with clustered crafts in front and the picturesque acclivities of the hills behind, is a place that always looks quite tolerable to live in, which is more than I can think of some more prosperous burghs further up the river. To its west stands the rocky promontory of Dunglass, on which survive few remnants of the castle which was once a stronghold of the Clan Colquhoun. Dunglass Castle, as a junior warden to Dumbarton in command of the passage of the Clyde, played its own part in our civil wars, and might have been a staunch old "biggin'" yet were it not for the shameless custom of elected persons to make quarries of their noblest monuments. In the middle of the eighteenth century, the commissioners of Dumbarton—now dead under inadequate tombstones, which do not publish their folly in life—sanctioned the demolition of the castle, and applied the freestone to the repair of the neighbouring quay, a barbarity only checked in 1812, when Archibald Buchanan, ancestor of the present owner, acquired the estate and partially restored the disappearing structure. On the highest part of the promontory now there stands an obelisk to the memory of Henry Bell.

Leaving Bowling, we are at the inner end of the estuary, and, seen at low tide, it makes no great demand on the imagination to believe one looks on an ebbed fiord that has lost most of its power to fill again. Bleak areas of ooze lie between the now ar-separate shores, and the navigable water is an attenuate stream whose course, for the pilot steering through high tide which covers the muddy banks, lending them a specious look of safety, is marked by numberless lights and beacon towers. Once, no doubt, the terraces on the shores were sea-cliffs fringed with wood, and the rocks proclaim the vigour of the flood that beat on them. Geologists have had what seems a ghoulish satisfaction in dwelling on the meaning of this strange recession—they have seen in the far future a Clyde devoid of estuary altogether, reduced to a rivulet or deepened to a dead canal. The Vale of Leven, behind Dumbarton Rock, is a reclaimed swamp, and a depression of thirty feet would admit sea water to Loch Lomond; the parks of Erskine and Cardross are made of the accumulated soil of yesterday, which an inundation of twenty feet would restore again to the dominion of the sea. Acres, miles, and whole parishes of arable land have been gained, but the river itself is disappearing "from the midst of the earth." In one alarming passage, Hately Waddel asks us to contemplate from Lunderston Hill, below the Cloch, on a calm day at low tide, the Firth in front of the Bullwood of Dunoon, when we shall see "the commencement of an elliptical or horse-shoe fall, marked by the ripple of the water on a ledge of rocks underneath, which at last, like Connel Ferry on Loch Etive, if the recession of the ocean does not cease, will be impassable." It may be so, but there are still fifty odd fathoms of good salt sea

LOW TIDE AT DAYBREAK, DUMBARTON ROCK

opposite Dunoon, and we can afford to regard the very remote prospect with equanimity.

East of the plain on which Dumbarton Rock stands guardian of Lennox, there is a loftier eminence, that, in contrast with the bare berg of Dumbarton, presents a most entrancing sylvan aspect—Dumbuck, a buttress of the Kilpatrick hills, wooded almost to its summit. It commands a glorious prospect, from Tinto to Arran and from the Grampians to Ayrshire, but—more practically, no doubt, to the view of Prince Charles Edward's forces in 1745, who occupied it ineffectually—it also commands Dumbarton itself. Between Dumbuck and Dumbarton an artist would not hesitate to choose the former, yet the castled rock, that stray and stranded brother of Ailsa and the Bass, which jumps to the eye a little too insistently to be resolved into, and harmonised with, its immediate environment, has a history that peculiarly endears it even to Scotsmen who may never have set foot on it. That dark, intractable basalt mass, seen from passing ships or from the railway on the opposite side of the estuary, has given to many of us in the West our first real lesson in Scottish history, since it made us feel emotionally the narrow bounds in which our country's ancient strife was usually conducted; made us realise the value of pass and warden tower; made real for us the tale of the epileptic in the escalade, and generally recovered our country's story from the realm of myth and faery. It is an imperishable monument to divers races, dynasties, and ideals, and to countless nameless and forgotten men. Theodosia—Balclutha—Castrum Arthuri—Urbs Legionis—Dunbreatan—perchance at eve when the valley fills with dusk, part smoke and darkness, part an exhalation of the marsh and river, the rock, which at various times has had these names, cries some slogan to the shades, and from plutonian shores, Northern Valhalla, or Christian paradise or purgatorial fires, come the responsive ghosts of men whose ecstasies and agonies, faiths and fervours were in life centred sometime on this pinnacle of the sea.

In such a muster would be the vague wild creatures of crannog and barrow, Pict, Celt, Briton—what you will; Roman legionaries and Tungrian auxiliaries, Scandinavian sea-rovers, heathen Saxons, English and French invaders, cut-throat Scottish revolutionaries, psalm-singing Covenanters, for all of them in their day and generation have looked with "wild surmise" or scraped their shins upon that dour unimpressionable crag. Rhydderch Hael, first King of the Cumbria whereof it was the capital should be there; Eadberct and Angus MacFergus who sacked and burned it, Olaf the White who subdued it by famine, Wallace who was its prisoner, Bruce who (they say) captured it almost single-handed, Mary Queen of Scots who sailed from it as a child to France and visited it again in 1563,—wraiths of them must surely haunt that lonely rock against which fleets and armies have been drawn. Now "I have seen the walls of Balclutha, but they were desolate. The fire had resounded in the halls,

CRAIGENDORAN, FROM ARDMORE

and the voice of the people is heard no more. The stream of Clutha was removed from its place by the fall of the walls. The thistle shook there its lonely head: the moss whistled to the wind. The fox looked out from the windows, the rank grass of the wall waved round its head." So Fingal sang—or more probably Mr. James Macpherson,—but one need go to Dumbarton now neither for pomp of war nor solitude and silence. Even in the days of Coleridge he could not get sleeping in Dumbarton inn because of its noise, and the din of industry has vastly increased about the rock since then. The rock is, if anything, an obstruction to profitable business; no longer does the War Office pretend to maintain it as a garrison though the Act of Union insists on its careful preservation, and it has even been denuded of the mighty brand we used to look upon with reverence as truly "Wallace's sword." And yet, but for the rock, Dumbarton of to-day, canopied by the smoke of factories, chequered by the poles and frames of shipyards, dumping ground of late for some of the largest and ugliest "works" in the West, would not be at all attractive. Its early history is, of course, inextricably interwoven with that of the castle: it has been a free Royal Burgh since 1222; in 1490 it was the chief naval station for Scotland, its harbour at the confluence of the River Leven giving shelter from the storms of nature and its rock immunity from the hazards of war. Over their toddy, old Dumbarton burgesses of a former generation rued bitterly the lack of civic prescience which made the corporation of the seventeenth century refuse the opportunity they were offered, of making their town the port of Glasgow. Like Greenock, it for generations imposed a toll on passing vessels, and till recent times its ships were exempt from all dues at the Broomielaw and other wharves of Glasgow.

To-day the leading industry in Dumbarton is shipbuilding. There are two eminent and long-established firms—M'Millan & Son and the firm founded by William Denny in the early part of last century. Associated with Napier, Denny did more than any of his contemporaries to establish the shipbuilding prestige of the Clyde, and the firm still maintains its reputation as among the greatest and most successful in the world. It was from a small and unpretentious yard that William Denny launched the steamer *Marjory* of 1815 to astonish the British navy in the Downs where no such craft had ever been seen before: from an enormous and intricate area of yard, engine shop, wet dock and experimental tank, successive Dennys (William left seven sons, all bred to the business) have contributed ships to the fleets of the great carrying companies.

If one makes chairs one must make chips, and the outfall of Loch Lomond, the Leven which Pennant described as "unspeakably beautiful" and Smollett apostrophised as

"Pure stream, in whose transparent wave
My youthful limbs I wont to lave,"

HELENSBURGH, FROM THE GOLF LINKS

having been soiled irremediably by the print-fields and dyeworks of the "Vale," loses the last relic of its Arcadian origin when it passes into the shadow of Dumbarton rock. Old Cardross village faced Dumbarton on the other bank of Leven, and beside it was the castle which was the favourite residence, and the deathplace of King Robert the Bruce, but no stone of the building stands above the turf of the knoll on which ceased to beat that gallant heart the Douglas hurled among the Saracens.

Though the Cardross of Bruce was on Leven bank, the modern village of that name is further down the Clyde, from which the railway separates it. Built on an expansive terrace stolen from the sea, its villa gardens and its neighbouring fields are crowded with sea-channel and shells. Ardmore, a mile-long promontory with a wooded knoll at the outer end of it and a mansion house, thrusts out to the west of it like a fist defying Greenock over the way. Cardross marks the limit of the jurisdiction of the Clyde Navigation Trust. It is a pleasant leafy walk to Helensburgh, the prosperous town of ease which curves for two miles round the bay near the Gareloch mouth. There is a certain air—not strictly speaking, hauteur, let us call it dignity or self-respect,—about Helensburgh which makes it stand aloof from the vulgar competition of other coast towns for popular recognition. It does not advertise itself as the "Madeira of Scotland," and, following the counsel of Fénelon, does "everything without excitement, simply in the spirit of grace."

Probably the only ungraceful feature of it is its name, and that was well meant by the gallant husband, the Colquhoun who founded the town in 1776. He seems to have had some dream of making it a place of commerce, for "bonnet-makers, stocking, linen, and woollen weavers" were specially invited to settle in it, but treadles and shuttles have never figured much in the industry of Helensburgh, and after years of slow growth, it smirches heaven with no factory smoke, and comes as near as we can boast on the estuary to a "garden town." With a plate-glass front of shops and tenements to the sea, its back parts are laid out in rectangular boulevards and villas smothered in foliage. Marvellous roses grow there; the summer may be somewhat ardent, but in winter and spring the air is singularly bland.

In recent years Helensburgh has climbed from the sea-wall to the braes behind it, where the West Highland railway meanwhile seems to check its aspirations. Men retired from the fever and fret of Glasgow have here taken unto them rural homes, but not so rural that there shall not be shops, telephones, good schools and the chance of an occasional classic concert; others, less fortunate, but ambitious of Mr. Yeats's nine bean-rows and the hive for the honey bee, travel to and from Glasgow daily, on a railway service of about forty minutes which may be blissfully hastened to the mind by the delusive joys of Nap. A folding card-table is, or was, a common part of the equipment of many compartments in the

LAST DAYS OF C.T.S. "CUMBERLAND,"

Burned by the boys off Row, Gareloch

"business train" from the city in the afternoon. The allusion to classic concerts is indicative of culture; chamber and orchestral concerts which the much larger community of Greenock painfully disregard are almost invariably a success in Helensburgh. Painters, too, have favoured it; there is no "Helensburgh School" it is true, but studios hide among its flowers, and an infinite number of notable pictures have been inspired by the hills, shores, and sylvan lanes of its neighbourhood. Colin Hunter spent his youth here, and learned to love and paint the sea; Milne Donald lived here in his closing years, selling his pictures for a fraction of what they fetched in after years. Alexander Fraser, David Murray, and Alfred East have pitched their easels here in successive seasons, and Sir James Guthrie painted much of his "Highland Funeral" in the studio of a distinguished Helensburgh amateur.

A somewhat forlorn pier keeps Helensburgh to some extent in touch with its neighbour towns on the Firth, but there is no harbour, and the bulk of the railway traffic for the coast is from Craigendoran, a station and pier at its extreme eastern boundary. The busy Greenock roadstead with its varied shipping adds to the interest of Helensburgh's days; the further lights of towns on the Firth give its nights a hint of distant festival. And though the burgh is, in a generous sense, a suburb of Glasgow, it is in sweet communicable relation with the wilds, for the road behind it climbs upward to the sombre lonely beauty of Glen Fruin, and Loch Lomond is only five miles distant. "All that is beautiful, indeed, of earth, or sea, or sky," says Hugh Macdonald with his customary emphasis, "may be said to be congregated round this favoured spot, and rejoices the hearts of its summer visitants."

To the west of Helensburgh, and between it and the embowered old village of Row, is Ardencaple, which was long the dowager home of the Argylls, who owned both sides of the entrance to the Gareloch. In this old Scottish baronial castle the late Duke of Argyll was born and spent a cloistered youth. But Ardencaple was really but a modern acquisition of the Campbell chiefs; of old it was the home of the Macaulays, true "children of the mist," a sept of the Clan Macgregor. Row village, round a little bay from Ardencaple, was, long before Sir James Colquhoun laid out the plans for Helensburgh, the chief place in the parish. It is a sweet spot in a "lown" nook of a long low point of land which here constricts the Gareloch. The kirk tower dominates it; the heresy of a former incumbent of the kirk has unhappily associated the name of Row irrevocably with a clerical dispute that may have meant much to the good folk of the time but looks singularly petty in retrospect.

On the opposite side of the narrow strait, Rosneath village, rustic and sequestered, retains all the solemn peace of an earlier age. The inn at the pier was designed by the Princess Louise, and prepares the

ROW

visitor for picturesque things to follow; he is not disappointed, though the picturesque charm of Row is due to nature and simplicity. Its avenue of ancient yew trees is perhaps the finest in the country; two enormous silver firs, contorted and distended, make you doubt if abnormality in arboreal antiquity is, sentiment apart, any more desirable than in the human world. In the quiet old churchyard of Rosneath Dugald Stewart's father ministered, and the Storys, of which the younger was Principal of Glasgow University. Dean Stanley loved to walk in the yew tree avenue and meditate among the tombs. The fiction of Scott sent Jeanie Deans to Rosneath; Blind Harry credits the place with some characteristic adventures on the part of William Wallace; tradition asserts that Balfour of Burley, the assassin of Archbishop Sharpe, ended his own days here under a disguised name; and George IV., visiting the Duke of Argyll at the handsome House of Rosneath, expressed an interest in the illicit whisky which at the time was briskly manufactured in the "Whistler Glen," and the Duke with difficulty procured him some—a dubious courtesy, since the product of the smugglers' still has ever been, despite romance, a fearsome beverage. In the parish of Rosneath, but on the other side of the peninsula, near the mouth of Loch Long, are Kilcreggan and Cove, two of the sunniest villages of the Firth.

CHAPTER XIV

GREENOCK

Per me si va nella Città dolante.

"*We* have not passed into a doleful City,
We who were led to-day down a grim dell,
By some too boldly named 'the Jaws of Hell!'
Where be the wretched ones, the sights for pity?
These crowded streets resound no plaintive ditty:—
As from the hive where bees in summer dwell,
Sorrow seems here excluded; and that knell,
It neither damps the gay nor checks the witty.
Alas! too busy Rival of old Tyre,
Whose merchants Princes were, whose decks were thrones;
Soon may the punctual sea in vain respire
To serve thy need, in union with that Clyde
Whose nursling current brawls o'er mossy stones,
The poor, the lonely, herdsman's joy and pride!"

So Wordsworth, melancholy prophetic, wrote of Greenock in one of his "Itinerary Sonnets." He must have seen it under the most favourable auspices, for Greenock, despite graces that reveal themselves on better acquaintance, presents no such happy countenance to the casual passer-by. Its very name,

WEST HARBOUR, GREENOCK

which signified, in hybrid Gaelic-Norse, a "sunny bay," suggests some irony, since it is for rain the place is now climatically celebrated, and the visitor who threads its central streets finds that neither sorrow nor plaintive ditty is rigorously excluded from our western Tyre. Though Greenock, as we see it to-day, is a growth of little more than a century, its roots are deep in time. St. Laurence is its patron saint; the mediaeval hamlet, which has mention in the Ragman's Roll, doubtless gathered round the chapel of St. Laurence, which stood at the west of Virginia Street, and the bay in front bore St. Laurence's name. The Shaws, who were the landlords, and the ancestors of Sir Hugh Shaw Stewart, superior of the town, obtained a charter from Charles I. conferring on it the rights and privileges of a burgh of barony in 1635. A stone pier was built, sheltering a little fleet of fishing smacks and open boats which traded with Ireland and the Isles, further foreign adventure being a privilege of royal burghs alone. The little burgh flourished on the herring, which, in the Gaelic proverb, lives "on the foam of its own tail," and in the latter part of the seventeenth century did an enormous fishery trade, directed by a company styled "Royal," since Charles II. was a shareholder. In 1674 over 20,000 barrels of herring were sent to La Rochelle alone, and the brand of Greenock was as popular on the Baltic as the brand of Castlebay,. Barra, is to-day.

The early part of the eighteenth century found the burgesses ambitious of extension; the government would give no help in the formation of a harbour, and the inhabitants, at the instigation of Sir John Shaw, built one at their own expense "a most commodious, safe and good harbour, having 18 feet depth at high tide." So rapidly did the trade increase thereafter that Greenock was made the principal customs station on the Clyde, a precedence hitherto possessed by Port-Glasgow. Later in the century, parliament, impressed by the independent enterprise of Sir John and his feuars, to augment the facilities of the port, sanctioned a levy of twopence on the pint of ale or beer brewed for sale, brought in or tapped within the town and county—a common device of the period for making Scottish burgesses drink to their own good luck. The purely feudal management of the burgh terminated and popular representation took its place. Greenock throve. The little row of thatched cottages near the water spread cannily; landward folks and foreigners from the misty Highlands came to its booths shopping; among them, more than once, no doubt, Rob Roy, though mostly on peaceful missions. It was really in pursuit of his profession, however, he took advantage of the absence of Sir John Shaw and his fighting tail during the Jacobite rising of 1715, to make a raid on the south shore of the Clyde between Greenock and Erskine Ferry, and collect a nice selection of lowland cattle. The man had undoubted genius as tactician; his enterprise not only involved an entrance "all boden in fier of warre" among thriving and well

C.T.S. "EMPRESS," FORMERLY
H.M.S. "REVENGE"

populated villages, but the transportation of the stolen bestial by boats, and naval manoeuvring was hardly his province. He requisitioned *vi et armis* all the boats on the Dumbarton shore, ferried his loot across the Clyde and up the Leven to Loch Lomond, and drove it on its own feet thereafter to Balquhidder. A hundred Greenock men, assisted by men and arms from a 74-gun ship in the roads, pursued the caterans but succeeded only in recapturing the boats. It was probably with a poignant memory of this visitation that Greenock in 1745 raised a company of volunteers for the defence of the neighbourhood, but luckily its active services in the campaign of the Young Chevalier were not required.

The town no longer lived on the herring that figured in its ancient civic motto; it developed a great foreign shipping trade; gained renown in sugar refining, rope-spinning, sail-making, ship-building. The quays extended; the population vastly increased; money flowed through it like the Delling burn that brawled with a muddy crest out into the East India Harbour. Cartsdyke, a little old community with one street and a harbour, found itself jostled by its growing neighbour, and has long since lost its personal identity. It was from Cartsdyke wharf—on the other side of the Delling and Carts burns—that some of the vessels engaged in the ill-fated Darien expedition took their departure in 1696 with more money than poor Scotland could well spare. All the later and greater harbour works of

Greenock are there; they culminated, after half a century of the most daring and successful development, in the James Watt Dock, which was expected to divert much of the shipping from Glasgow but has not realised the dreams of its projectors.

James Watt was born in Greenock, in a house which subsequently became a tavern. His father was a small shipowner and town councillor of the burgh. Greenock has few antiquities, and unhappily Samuel Smiles, seeking "local colour" for his "Lives of the Engineers," found the citizens had razed the home of their most notable townsman, and were indifferent to the site of it. But Greenock has honoured the name of Watt elsewhere than in its dock; a curious cairn to his memory is in the cemetery, and a commemorative statue by Chantrey is in the vestibule of the Watt Institution erected by his son.

If Greenock could appreciate scientific genius it has ever had a name for indifference to poetry. John Wilson, the author of the most ambitious poem inspired by the river Clyde, was appointed a schoolmaster in the burgh on condition that he should "abjure the profane and unprofitable art of poem-making." "I once thought to live by the breath of fame," wrote the involuntary mute inglorious bard, years after, "but how miserably was I disappointed, when, instead of having my performance applauded in crowded theatres, and being caressed by the great—for what will not a poetaster, in the intoxicating delirium of possession dream!—I was condemned to bawl myself to hoarseness among wayward brats, to cultivate sand, and wash Ethiopians, for all the dreary days of an obscure life, the contempt of shopkeepers and brutish skippers." Another poet who fared ill in "Sugaropolis" was poor Jean Adam of Cartsdyke, who in the early years of the eighteenth century taught "wayward brats" as Wilson did, and wrote religious verse in the Tate and Brady style that scarce supports the claim advanced for her authorship of "There's nae luck aboot the Hoose," which Burns declared "one of the most beautiful songs in the Scots or any other language." Whether she or William Julius Mickle wrote that moving lyric still remains a point disputed; the association of her name with it has rendered the more pathetic her neglected and homeless fate which ended in a Glasgow poorhouse. Nor is the obloquy of the bard in Greenock completed with the case of this poor school-mistress; Thomas Campbell sent the manuscript of his "Hohenlinden" to a Greenock newspaper (as the story goes), and had it returned to him as not being up to the journal's standard for things of the kind.

In our own day, another poet, and probably the greatest we have had in Scotland for a century, has had scholastic relations with Greenock. John Davidson spent his youth here, and "washed Ethiopians" with as little taste for it as Wilson. He has in his ballad on "The Making of a Poet" painted Greenock as no artist has done in pigment.

The Clyde

"I need," he says, "no world more spacious than the region here—

"The foam-embroidered firth, a purple path
For argosies that still on pinions speed,
Or fiery-hearted cleave with iron limbs
And bows precipitate the pliant sea;
The sloping shores that fringe the velvet tides
With heavy bullion and with golden lace
Of restless pebble woven and fine spun sand;
The villages that sleep the winter through,
And, waking with the spring, keep festival
All summer and all autumn: this grey town
That pipes the morning up before the lark
With shrieking steam, and from a hundred stalks
Lacquers the sooty sky; where hammers clang
On iron hulls, and cranes in harbours creak,
Rattle and swing, whole cargoes on their necks;
Where men sweat gold that others hoard or spend,
And lurk like vermin in their narrow streets:
This old grey town, this firth, the further strand
Spangled with hamlets, and the wooded steeps,
Whose rocky tops behind each other press,
Fantastically carved like antique helms
High-hung in heaven's cloudy armoury,
Is world enough for me. Here daily dawn
Burns through the smoky east; with fire-shod feet
The sun treads heaven, and steps from hill to hill
Downward before the night that still pursues
His crimson wake; here winter plies his craft,
Soldering the years with ice; here spring appears,
Caught in a leafless brake, her garland torn,
Breathless with wonder, and the tears half dried
Upon her rosy cheek; here summer comes

And wastes his passion like a prodigal
Right royally; and here her golden gains
Free-handed as a harlot autumn spends,
And here are men to know, women to love."

Fervent though Mr. Davidson's verse may be, it in no way (barring the absence of any adequate allusion to rain) overestimates the wonderful variety of natural charm in the environment. From the terraced streets that rise on the heights behind the generous esplanade, the vision, passing over the evidences of reeking and unremitting toil, compasses the sparkling firth, the Highland lochs and hills. Pennant was enraptured with the prospect, which from the Lyle Road or the "Cut" reveals parts of seven or eight counties. John Galt, the first and greatest of our "kailyarders," must have often looked across the firth "broad-bosomed like a mere," with some effect on subsequent emotion, for he spent the most impressionable period of his life in Greenock, and though he once protested that he could not recollect a single circumstance that should endear the place to him, he later changed his mind. "Much of my good nature towards mankind," he said, "is assuredly owing to my associates at Greenock," and it was back to Greenock he came, a broken man, to die. A curious thing is Scottish sentiment; though Greenock has duly commemorated Galt, it is not to his grave the public make their pilgrimages, but to that of Burns's "Highland Mary," who is buried in the old kirkyard.

Through grey, strenuous and constricted thoroughfares giving glimpses of the harbours—" deep-drawing barks do there disgorge their fraughtage"—one enters the district of Cartsdyke and passes to the burgh of Port-Glasgow, three miles distant. The shipyard and engineering works of Caird & Co., between the Albert and West Harbours, is in Greenock proper. Founded by the father of Principal Caird of Glasgow, and Edward Caird, the Master of Balliol, who were born here, it passed to the hands of the father of the present Cairds, a distant relative who had served his apprenticeship in the yard, and was afterwards to give it a prominent place in the shipbuilding world. In Cartsdyke, Scott & Co.'s yard, managed for several generations by the same family, and one of Russell's yards, contribute enormously to the shipping output of the Clyde, of which Russell & Co. have for years had the lion's share, vastly exceeding the production of any other shipyard on any part of the river.

Port-Glasgow owes its existence to the commercial spirit and enterprise of Glasgow merchants, who, refused the privilege of establishing a harbour either at Dumbarton or Troon, bought thirteen acres of land in Newark Bay in 1668, laid out the ground for a town, and built a harbour. It was made a free port and the principal customs station on the Clyde. The first dry and graving dock in Scotland was erected there in 1762, by which time the port was sending singularly unlucky whalers to the Greenland seas, and American, West Indian, and continental ships were crowding to its quays. Port-Glasgow grew

PORT-GLASGOW FROM CARDROSS

rapidly beyond the limits originally contemplated, and the fishermen's huts, which formed the old village of Newark, became absorbed within its boundaries. But its supremacy as a shipping centre terminated with the wakening of Greenock, and the deepening of the upper Clyde; its trade declined alarmingly, only to be restored, and of a different character, with the start of steam navigation. It has a noisy and unkempt prosperity that is due to such yards as Russell & Co.'s, and Rodger's, and various activities more or less of a marine complexion. Mournfully, and outwith the bounds of the encroaching shipyards, stands old Newark Castle, contemplating a fashion of life so different from that with which, five hundred years ago, it was familiar. More a place of residence than a fortified stronghold, Newark Castle was probably built by the Maxwells of Danyelstoun in the second half of the fifteenth century. The more modern and by far the greater part of it was probably built in 1597-99 by the Sir Patrick Maxwell whose monogram is on the window heads and tympanum of the entrance door. There was also a chapel and endowed chaplainry to the barony of Finlaystoun Maxwell or Newark, the site of which is pointed out near the castle, but all traces of it have been obliterated by the shipbuilding yards, which have left but a slender strip of ground round the castle itself. The castle ceased to be inhabited by its owners in the beginning of the eighteenth century, and thus subsequently fell somewhat into decay internally. Sir Hugh Shaw

Stewart, the present owner, takes some interest in it, however, and keeps it in weather-tight condition.

Greenock in its leisure hours, however, but rarely takes the Rue-end road to the "Port"; it much prefers the breezier way to Gourock, two miles further down the firth, with its older and more poetic memories. For kings have sailed from Gourock, a circumstance which has had less influence on its history than the discovery that herring could be cured by smoke. The first red herrings known in Britain were here produced in 1688. Railed in on the highest terrace of the promontory round both sides of which the burgh hangs, is a rough, grey boulder to which old passing mariners paid superstitious respect. To-day their sirens hoot derisively, and "Granny Kempoch" does not care, mysterious and serene in her incongruous surroundings.

GOUROCK

CHAPTER XV

THE GARELOCH AND LOCH LONG

The lochs confer on the estuary of the Clyde features of interest, beauty, and romance possessed by no other great maritime river in the kingdom. It is a vista of melancholy grey mud-banks that the seaman opens as he steers his vessel past the crimson lightship at the Nore into the muddy efflux of the Thames, with no distinctive landmarks to the eye; the Humber, the Tyne, the Forth, and Tay of eastern inlets, and the Bristol Channel and the Mersey on the west, meet the traffic of the oceans more or less abruptly; as genially as the Clyde perhaps, but with no bewitching fiords and mountain corridors such as seem to offer irresistible alternatives to the mariner who has passed the dome of Ailsa Craig and seeks the shortest way to Glasgow. Ships have found this picturesque approach not wholly free from perils, and there have been those that, native-born, have sailed out of our estuary to be absent for years on alien seas, and met destruction on their first return, upon the homely Ayr or Cumbrae shores, for Nature has no memory or no heart. Yet the bold outlines of the coast help to a good landfall; the wide portals of the sea between the Corsewall light and the Sanda open hospitably; the bending channels, lit lavishly by towns and beacons, or clamant in fogs with siren and bell, can be traversed with a certain immunity from every gale that blows, and the Clyde is rich in sheltering havens.

It is this feature of generous shelter, combined with deep water, that has made the estuary a little too popular, for the landsman's taste, with the owners of unemployed merchantmen and obsolete men-of-war. When freights fall, and big liners are withdrawn from the sea highways to "rest" like jaded actresses, they are moored in the Gareloch, with no improvement on the outlook from the villas of Row and Rosneath; when the Admiralty in saucy moods decides that certain types of battleship are no longer good enough to have the honour of a flag, they are dumped with pathetic lack of ceremony on the Holy Loch or Kyles of Bute to await their appointed doom at the hands of the breaker-up. We are flattered by such confidence but are prone to think it costs too much of natural beauty, spoiled—though but for a space—by the presence of untaxed discordant empty hulls from other waters or by the rusty relics of naval iron-mongery. The lochs, somehow, to our notion, seem to have some claim to be considered sacrosanct against commerce in its more obtrusive forms; at least the merchant ships that make the fortunes of people

THE GARELOCH

elsewhere appear intruders upon scenes which in their natural aspects are peculiarly dear to us. The old *Empress* training ship off Helensburgh no one has ever objected to, indeed that chequered oaken hull is an ornament to the roadstead, but we count ourselves lucky when the Gareloch is vacant of idle merchant steamers.

The first of the lochs to open up for the passenger going down the estuary, is Gareloch, between the promontory of Rosneath (which Scott in "The Heart of Midlothian" proclaimed an island) and the mainland of Dumbarton. Gareloch is small enough in area to comply with those curious canons of lake beauty which were authoritatively laid down by the chief of the Lake Poets. "In Scotland," wrote the mightily fastidious Wordsworth, "the proportion of diffused water is often too great. In most of the lakes this is the case. . . . It is much more desirable that lakes for the purpose of pleasure should be numerous and small and middle-sized than large, not only for communication by walks and rides, but for variety, and for recurrence of similar appearances." Gareloch, which unhappily he never saw, would surely have met with his kind approval, since it is considerably less than Ullswater. Along its western side, that starts at the wooded policies of Rosneath, on which is situated an "Italianate" castle owned by the Argylls, a chain of moorland hills of no great height extends, separating it from the parallel Loch Long; on the east more rounded summits culminate in a height of a thousand feet midway between Helensburgh and Garelochead. Low heathy hills are at the top, with the giant mountains of Argyllshire overlooking them. In the affections of Glasgow, Gareloch has never been a rival to its compeers on the Firth; it has only one considerable village at its upper end though there are piers at intervals that minister to a fringe of scattered mansions, villas, and cottages along both shores, and it wholly lacks the semi-urban features which the Glasgow masses love on holiday. For all that, its shady roads, silent beaches, and woody slopes are none the worse to the minds of those who know the Gareloch and ever return gladly to its peace.

Yet it was, curiously enough, on the Gareloch, that Glasgow, half-a-century ago, made its first attempt to outrage the sanctity of the Highland Sabbath, and the Colquhouns of Luss with their retainers vainly fought against the first incursion of trippers from a Sunday steamer. Time has been on the side of the Colquhouns; there have been no Sunday steamers on Gareloch for two or three generations; but Shandon, where there is a hydropathic, once the residence of Robert Napier the engineer, is, *per contra*, one of the two or three places in Scotland where Sunday golf is tolerated. The Colquhouns of Luss fought a more serious fight in an earlier age, and the name of Glenfruin has all to itself a bloody rubric in Highland history. To the north of the lands of Luss were the glens and corries sheltering the Macgregors. In a foray on a winter day in 1603, that fierce and

THE FERRY INN, ROSNEATH

lawless tribe, headed by its chief Alasdair Macgregor, ambushed the Colquhouns at a place by the Fruin Burn, three miles from Garelochhead, and the result in the long run proved as fatal for the victors as for the vanquished. The Colquhouns lost a hundred and forty men, and their lands were fired and pillaged. A party of students whom curiosity had led from Dumbarton to the scene of the engagement are said to have perished in the retreat, but this detail is not enumerated in the indictments against the Macgregors, whose utter extirpation now became the most passionate purpose of the government. By Acts of Parliament it was made a capital crime to bear the name Macgregor, or to give food or shelter to any of that tribe. Alasdair might well have cried in the words of Scott:

> "If they rob us of name and pursue us with beagles,
> Give their roofs to the flame and their flesh to the eagles."

Captured by a stratagem of the Earl of Argyll, he was hanged at Edinburgh—stipulating, with Highland vanity, for a foot or two of eminence above his henchmen on the scaffold—and his head for a season made a bonny ornament on the tolbooth walls of Dumbarton. Only that Macgregor who could prove that he had slain one of his own kinsmen of equal degree with himself was exempt from a vengeance that scourged and branded the inoffensive child and sent the boy to the scaffold. This policy of extermination lasted for generations. It was at or after the period of Shakespeare, Bacon, and Buchanan!

No such tragedies have given gloomy memories to the mountains of Loch Long—the "Lake of Ships" as the Gaelic has it—which opens from the Firth between the peninsula of Rosneath and the promontory of Strone. The tribes fought there too; the accounts are still extant for depredations by the men of Athole in the seventeenth century, but the savage polity ceased on the greater part of the shores of Loch Long generations before robber clans and broken men gave rest to Glen Strae and Glen Sloy. The charm of Loch Long perhaps most markedly reveals itself, not from the deck of a steamer, but from the shore at some inner reach of its deep indent. I prefer myself to see it on an autumn day from the height at Whistlefield, for there—the Gareloch, lovely but a little tame, left a mile or two behind—this nobler fiord comes suddenly to the vision with a shock of happy contrast. Its salt dark waters seem in such an hour a personal first discovery, untraversed and stainless, prisoners of the sleepless hills which they reflect with all their hues. So profound the surface then, it seems on a lower plane than the familiar sea, a glimpse of some waterway in a nether world, not "sad Acheron of Sorrow," for the hills are happy, but still remote, and half unreal. It is sad to find that Mr. and Mrs. Joseph Pennell, in their "Journey to the Hebrides," seem to have been ferried across Loch Long without retaining a single joyous memory

THE YEW AVENUE, ROSNEATH

of the experience. More lucky was the poet Rogers, who, coming into the upper end of the loch by Tarbet from Loch Lomond, got that emotion which, "recollected in tranquillity," found expression later in his

> "Tarbet! thy shore I climbed at last,
> And through thy shady region passed,
> Upon another shore I stood
> And looked upon another flood:
> Old Ocean's self! ('tis he who fills
> That vast and awful depth of hills)."

It has been by the Tarbet route indeed that most distinguished visitors have come to Loch Long, but seeing only the top end of it, and plunging almost immediately into the recesses of Glen Croe on their way further west, they have probably missed as much as Mr. and Mrs. Pennell. Coming to it this way the Wordsworths saw a sea loch for the first time and were a little disappointed. Coleridge had got tired of the jaunting-car and had just left them in that feckless and impolite way the poets of the period seemed to cultivate; "perhaps," says Dorothy, "had we been in a more cheerful mood of mind we might have seen everything with a different eye. The stillness of the mountains, the motion of the waves, the streaming torrents, the sea-birds, the fishing-boats were all melancholy; yet still, occupied as my mind was with other things, I thought of the long windings through which the waters of the sea had come to this inland retreat, visiting the inner solitudes of the mountains, and I could have wished to have mused out a summer's day on the shores of the lake. From the foot of these mountains whither might not a little barque carry one away? Though so far inland, it is but a slip of the great ocean; seamen, fishermen, and shepherds here find a natural home."

The shepherd has almost gone from the hills of Loch Long; the "larochs"—the sites of ruined cot and shealing—are sad memorials of more populous days in the shadow of Ben Arthur; even the tenure of the fisher is menaced, for the government have decided to open a torpedo-testing range in the waters parallel with the rugged peninsula long known in irony as Argyll's Bowling-Green, now christened Ardgoil, and lately gifted by a generous Glasgow man to his native city. The seamen Miss Dorothy alludes to have ever been a negligible quantity beyond the "hands" of pleasure steamer, yacht or gabbart; a cul-de-sac attracts no stately navies, though Hakon the Old of Norway sent some sixty of his galleys to this "Skipfjiord" in his final struggle for the Western Isles. The boats were "portaged" over the Tarbet Isthmus from Arrochar to Loch Lomond (Lokulofni of the Norse), whose shores and islands knew the havoc of viking brands. It was late in the year 1263; one of the gales that do not discompose the ships of our time strewed the strand of Loch Long with the wrecks of ten of Hakon's vessels.

Midway in its passage through the mountains, Loch Long throws to the north round Ardgoil peninsula

THE ROSE GARDEN, ROSNEATH HOUSE

an arm that takes the name Loch Goil. It is not the "dark and stormy" Loch Gyle of Campbell's poem, "Lord Ullin's Daughter," but it can be incomparably dark and stormy none the less, for the throat of Hell's Glen belches down the northern winds, and the alpine peaks of Ben Donich, Ben Lochan, Ben Reithe, Ben Bheula and Sgor Coinnich drag down the mists and rains. On the western side of the loch, Carrick Castle, a keep of the fifteenth century—maybe even older of foundation—presents a forlorn and crumbling front to a modern pier in grotesque propinquity. No scrap of story that I know of has survived to give the place the appeal of human intimacy: children were born there; men and women were its tenants; fires were in its hall; the pipe must have played there; tragedy must have stalked across its draw-bridge, long since non-existent; but all alike are whelmed in the inviolable mystery of Time. It is one of many ruined strongholds of Argyll and the West that so maintain a baffling taciturnity. The last and almost all we know with certainty of Carrick is that it was burned by the men of Athole carrying fire and sword through Cowal in the seventeenth century. Relics as old, perhaps, but less obtrusive to the eye of the passer by, and more informative, are to be found in the sculptured stones in the church of Lochgoilhead.

CHAPTER XVI

THE HOLY LOCH AND THE KYLES

When the stricter laws of quarantine prevailed upon the Clyde, the yellow flag of the lazaretto flew at the south-west end of the Holy Loch. To-day, the crafts that gather there are convened for pleasure only; the loch—which in truth is less a loch than a two mile bight or bay—is the rendezvous of yacht clubs, lively with regattas in summer, afforested with naked spars in the months of the yachtsman's hibernation. That this friendly bay should be Holy more than any other cove in its neighbourhood is a circumstance that has induced the most ingenious speculations of the topographist, but only two ascriptions need be noted here—that a vessel laden with sand from the Holy Land for the building of Glasgow Cathedral was stranded on these shores, or that the upper end of the loch was intimately associated in the mind of an earlier people with a pious atmosphere induced by the presence of a monkish cell which was founded there at the close of the sixth century by St. Fintan Mannu of Teach Mannu in Ireland. Church

ROSNEATH HOUSE
The seat of H.R.H. Princess Louise and the Duke of Argyll

place-names of the distinction of Kilfinan and Kilmun are not very common in Cowal; both of these possibly indicate the same saint, and there is something to be said for the theory of Dr. Cameron Gillies that the whole district of Cowal came under this one religious influence from Kilmun and its church. In any case piety has for many hundred years had tangible form on the Holy Loch, where the cell of Kilmun was succeeded in 1442 by a collegiate church founded by the first of the Argylls, Sir Duncan Campbell of Lochow, "for the soul's repose of Marjory his deceased wife, of his wife that now is, and of the deceased Celestine his first-born son." The Knight of Lochow was buried there in 1453, and it has ever since been the final resting place of the MacCailens Mor. Archibald the first Marquis lies there, with his head thrown into his coffin as an after-thought by warrant of Charles the Second after two or three years' "weathering" on the Tolbooth tower of Edinburgh, also his son who had a similar fate, and there too, "chapless, and knocked about the mazzard with a sexton's spade" lie the mortal elements of that Duchess Elizabeth of Hamilton and Argyll, who, as one of the "beautiful Miss Gunnings," turned the heads of London gallants a century and a half ago. "Here's fine revolution, an we had the trick to see't." All that is left of Duncan's chapel is a crumbling fragment of dreary looking tower in whose ivied cranny the swallow twitters and the night wind sighs.

A long, lofty rampart of heath-clad or pine-planted

hills flanks the northern shore of Holy Loch, rising abruptly from the snout of land called Strone, marching far inland to the junction of Glen Finnart with Loch Eck. On the opposite side hills more rounded and irregular rise from more generous beaches and culminate in the airy Bishop's Seat at a height of 1650 feet. At any part of the loch, almost, the views are singularly beautiful; Kilmun and Strone, which, with Blairmore round the corner in Loch Long, make one continuous fringe of dwellings for six or seven miles, look out on the morning sun, and a climb of no great hardship to the summit of Finnartmore is recompensed abundantly by the view it gives of spacious waters, islands, moors, and mountains, ships beating to the open sea, and smoking towns and hamlets. Till well on in the last century these shores were lonely, unfrequented; in 1829 David Napier, the engineer, whose name it is ill to escape from in any part of the Firth of Clyde, feued some fields in the neighbourhood of Kilmun church and built a row of villas which, known for ever after as "the canisters," give proof that engineering and architecture are very different arts. There was something almost uncanny in the prescient enterprise of the man who thus brought villadom to the Holy Loch. His home was at Glenshellish, a dozen miles away in a valley of Loch-Fyne; it is said to have been the first place in Cowal to which gravitation water was introduced, but more curious to his neighbours' eyes must have seemed the steam carriage with which, on the roads by Loch

LOCH LONG AND "THE COBBLER"

Eck, he anticipated the motor car by more than seventy years, and the iron steamer he placed on the lake.

Close though the head of Holy Loch is to the main traffic of the Firth, it has in its neighbourhood features of grandeur and solitude quite unknown to the multitudes who throng to Rothesay or Dunoon. If the view down the loch be lovely, it is upwards to the valleys that the artist has most often turned his eyes. Hugh Macdonald, the dear old garrulous cicerone of "Rambles round Glasgow" and "Days at the Coast," has in no way exaggerated the charms of the prospect I refer to: "Three mighty mountain glens," he says, "here converge and send down their tributary streams to the bosom of the loch—three vast and yawning glens, each flanked with a rugged and towering mountain range, here open their ponderous jaws sublime, and invite the wanderer into three separate regions of the wonderful. There is first the valley of the Eck, with its many-winding stream, leading through many a sweet and sylvan nook to the loch of the same name—a thing of beauty in its own way unexcelled—and from thence to Strachur and Loch Fyne. Then there is Glen Massan—with its fierce mountain torrent chafing into forms the most fantastic the everlasting rocks, and its terrible boundaries of huge overhanging peaks and ridges, the home of solitude, sublimity, and awe. Beyond, but still tributary to the Holy Loch, is Glen Lean, a wild and sterile gulf, but leading through its dim and shadowy recesses to the softer beauties which encircle the head of Loch Ridden. Three noble portals are they, and each accessible to the denizen of Kilmun."

The gifted Hugh has hardly spared me an adjective for these scenes, but I would, following in his footsteps, seek in Glen Massan no emotions of terror and the wild sublime, but a softer sentiment, roused by the forgotten Gaelic bard who sung the sorrows of the sons of Usnach ; and in Tarsuinn, Garrachra, and Glen Lean, I would restore, in fancy, shepherds and hunters on the grass-grown drove-road and the abandoned hill. The Clyde has drained these glens, not of their waters only, but of men, and melancholy broods among the shadows of Benmore as if it, too, remembered lonefully the unreturning generations.

"There's sorrow in the valley
  Where I have friends no more,
For lowly lies the rafter
  And the lintel of the door.
The friends are all departed,
  The hearth-stone's black and cold,
And sturdy grows the nettle
  On the place I loved of old.

O ! black might be that ruin
  Where my fathers dwelt so long,
And nothing hide the shame of it,
  The ugliness and wrong ;
The cabar and the corner-stone
  Might bleach in winds and rains,
But for the friendly nettle
  That took such a courtier's pains.

ROYAL CLYDE YACHT CLUB REGATTA,
HUNTER'S QUAY, JUNE, 1906

"Kariad" finishing first, "White Heather" winner

The Holy Loch and the Kyles

Here's one who has no quarrel
  With the nettle thick and tall,
That wraps the cheerless hearth-stone
  And screens the humbled wall,
That clusters on the footpath
  Where the children used to play,
And guards a household's sepulchre
  From all who come the way.

There's deer upon the mountain,
  There's sheep along the glen,
The forests hum with feather,
  But where are now the men?
Here's but the lowly *laroch*
  Where soft my footsteps fall,
My folks are quite forgotten
  And the nettle's over all."

The loneliness which has gone from the Holy Loch is still discoverable in Loch Striven and Loch Ridden, which, more daringly and through wilder mountain clefts, search deeper to the heart of lower Cowal. They thrust to the north from the curving Kyles of Bute, the channel which sunders Bute from the mainland, and has itself in parts the aspect of a lake. On the Clyde we have, I confess, a certain complacency about "the Kyles"; we do not brag of them since they were not of our making, but if you have not seen them, or having seen have not properly been impressed, you have our pity or contempt. The Kyles are the trump card of our finest summer steamers; to be going "a run down to the Kyles" is a morning prospect which makes even the

Glasgow stock-broker look particularly glad as he hurries to the station. And, indeed, that lovely arc of sea canal warrants, in almost any weather, all the glamorous thoughts its name arouses in the distant town. Trade has not stained a single stream that flows to it ; the hamlet of Colintraive and the little town of Tighnabruaich that doze on the marge of it but add to our pleasant recollections.

Loch Striven, the larger of the two lochs, leads north from the eastern entrance of the Kyles, gradually tapers from its mouth to its head, unlike most of the lochs, and runs for nine miles between steep and uniform hills. A farmhouse or a white-walled cottage rarely breaks the continuity of green braeside on either hand ; a church stands midway in a fold of hill ; the only road on the eastern bank lapses long before it has reached the top of the loch to a track but seldom travelled. In sunny weather, Striven shines with angelic benignance ; in gloomy days when the winds gulp down its gullies, it repels, and bids the burgesses of Rothesay, who look right up the throat of it, remember their macintoshes. Further west, Loch Ridden, thrusting midway from the Kyles, is much shorter but more picturesque though less solitary. A few flat islets at its mouth impede the passage ; on one of them called Eilean Dearg the Earl of Argyll in 1685 established a garrison which was meant to contribute to the discomfiture of James VII. There was an old tower on the islet ; some mounds were run up round it, and fortified

THE CLOCH

with cannon from the Earl's petty fleet of three vessels, and there were deposited the stores and ammunition upon which everything depended. The tiny garrison yielded the place, stores and all, to one or two English frigates, and the magazine was destroyed. Half way up Loch Ridden is the pier of Ormidale which tenuously attaches the few people of this valley of the sea with the busy outer world, and the head of the loch receives through sandy deltas the waters of the Ruel river that has come for miles through a lovely glen that is parallel with Loch Fyne.

CHAPTER XVII

YACHTING

All winter the yachts of the Firth lie "on the hard" snugly housed at Sandbank, Gourock, or some other friendly shelter where they rank in rows, grotesque imaginings of the naval architect, showing their wedge-shaped under-structures, bereft for the time of any hint of speed and grace. There and then, propped on their crutches, with the green paint flaking from their lower strakes, their white bulwarks fouled with dripping rains, their brass-work tarnished and their masts unstepped, they look pathetic, like Greenwich pensioners who will never again go back to sea. Kittiwakes, playing in south-west storms, come at times to the yards and stand on these mute helpless hulls, wondering perhaps to find them unresponsive to the summons of the breeze, the welcome of the wave, since they like themselves are birds—large beautiful birds whose plumage for whiteness and whose wings for power make them the princes and princesses of the flying summer world. Surely the sea wants them in these winter months ; the Sounds miss them ; the bays

THE GANTOCKS

feel lonely! Their men are far scattered; ploughing Hebridean crofts or hanging on frozen shrouds in other latitudes, servants of pleasure no more for a space, but counting the days till they shall return to the sport of kings. And their owners—they have suffered a sea-change; discarding emblematic buttons and pipe-clayed shoes they have become mere merchants with the pen in hand instead of the tiller.

But no sooner do the birds of the wood begin to build than those sea-birds, infected by the Spring, begin to stir; as the days lengthen they come flying forth and shake their wings in the heat of the sun, and grow bolder and stronger, till with the swallow they remember and soar into the old familiar blue. Then the Firth of Clyde is itself again, and standing on its shore you see these swooping vessels wheel and poise; as things all quivering with life, invested with some soul of reason. Of all the varied crafts that make the estuary a busy highway there are three that eminently delight the artist's eye—not the frequent ship of war with her sinister grey reptile aspect, nor the ocean liner like a tenement afloat, nor the great white steam yacht that is a palace, nor the sordid "tramp," but the square-rigged merchantman, the humble lighter, and the cutter yacht. The doom of the sailing ship is knelled, they say, but still white barques and brigantines rise day by day like phantoms of dead armadas and come round the Cloch as proud and stately as of old; their figure-heads stretch and aspire in ivory and gold as though only they knew the secret of the sea and are singing night and day as they lead the way over its unseen paths. Next to them I prize the little lighters—carriers of coal and coastal merchandise, whose broad up-lifting bows, squat funnels, thick short masts and derricks mass so often in a figure that recalls old galleys on Celtic tombs. Merchantman and lighter please by their lines alone, and some vague reminiscence they suspire; the yachts delight more by their life and spirit than by their lines. They must be in motion to appeal to us; with wings folded or becalmed, most of their grace is gone from them; lacking any arresting attitude of repose they seem to have no "decorative possibilities," and those high peaked white pinions compel our admiration only when they gather up the wind and fly by that clean and invisible agency.

When yachting began on the Firth may never be known with certainty. There were yachts and regattas here before any others of our countrymen, with the exception of a few enthusiasts in Cork had developed the pastime, but the actual beginning goes back far beyond the period when a trickle of history begins to flow from a morass of conjecture. It was not until Parliament under the Georges made stirring times for the coast by laying heavy import duties upon unwilling traders that yachting finds mention as a sport apart from the ordinary marine utilities. In those days the lower Firth, badly lit and insufficiently watched, sheltered many smuggling luggers, and when it became necessary to describe them to inquisitive revenue officers they were ranked with pleasure vessels of a

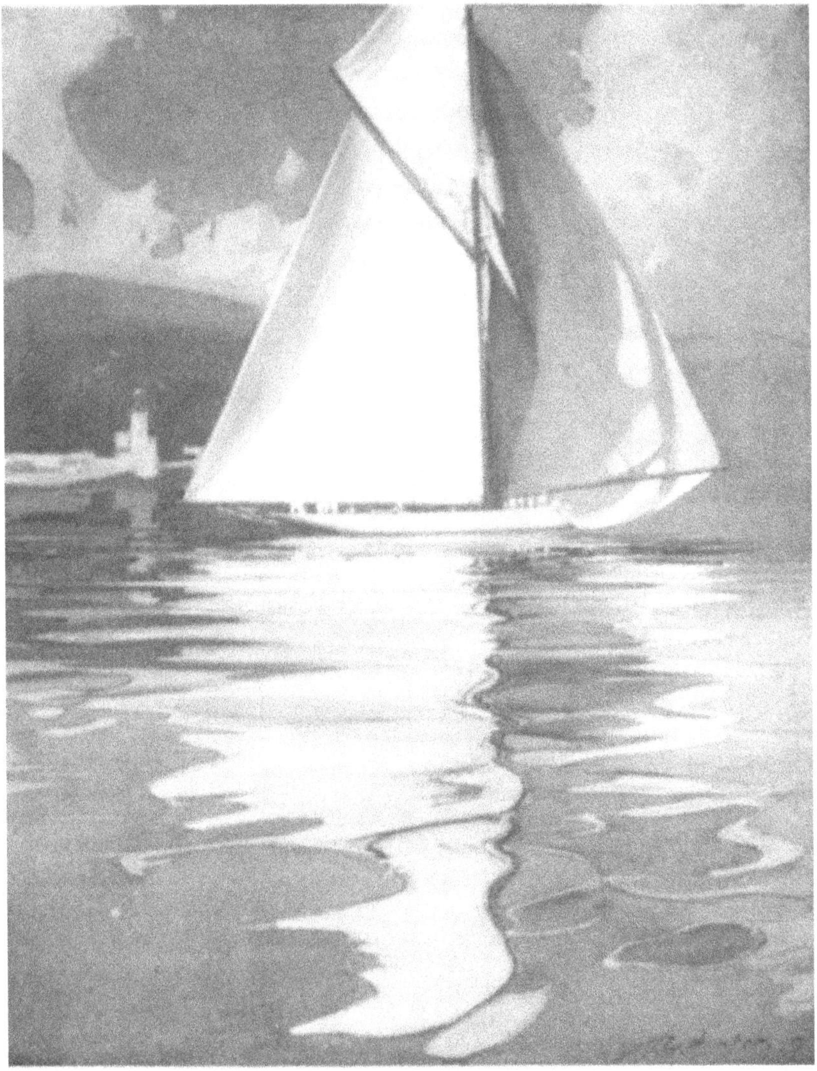

YACHT "KARIAD" PASSING "THE CLOCH" LIGHTHOUSE

more reputable kind. On their fleetness of foot they depended for safety, and in their efforts to build flying smugglers the old boat-builders laid the beginnings of a craft that has done something for the prosperity and much for the pleasure of the dwellers in the neighbourhood of Clyde. How their productions would rate if judged by the standards of to-day must remain unknown, but some of them had a reputation for speed that still survives. Such, for example, is the case of a French lugger which ran the gauntlet for years though known by sight to every gauger on the coast. She was captured at last, but fell with such a reputation that the Duke of Portland of the period had the crippled hull dissected for the purpose of having a racing yacht built on the same lines.

William IV. was still king, when, on a cruise which a number of yachting men of the Clyde made to Irish waters on board the *Melita*, owned by Mr. James Smith of Jordanhill, it was suggested that the sailing enthusiasts who made their headquarters in the Firth should form a club for the encouragement and development of the sport. The outcome of the proposal was the Royal Northern Yacht Club. They were staid old sportsmen in these days, and they took their sailing pastime in all seriousness. The King's Navy, still unspoiled by the introduction of the fireman and the coal-trimmer, and ruled by seamen instead of mechanics, was in the days of its prime, and it was in the wake of the navy that these Northern yachtsmen followed with humble pride. Flag officers were elected and endowed with all the powers and pomp that went with the corresponding ranks in the ships of the King. Some influence of those days can yet be traced in the quaint and punctilious etiquette which is maintained in the pastime. Instead of the generous area of the quarter deck of the old fighting ship, there may be only the circumscribed space and insecure footing afforded by the counter of the modern racer, but this is as sacred to the use of the owner and his guests as the "Admiral's walk" was to the autocrats of the three-deckers. The formalities which govern the use of the flags are, too, a study by themselves. The off-hand manners of the present day have cut a little into the reverence due to the Commodore of the fleet, but there is still a penalty for the owner so reckless of the proprieties as to join or leave the fleet without a salute to Commodore, or disregard the sunset gun with which the commodore vessel signals the lowering of all flags and the hoisting of anchor lights.

Although something of the old order has been preserved, much more has been lost, and it is only in the prints and rule books of the clubs that occasional glimpses of the old time club-life can be obtained. There is, for instance, a rule still nominally in force which provides that "members (except under particular circumstances) shall wear the uniform at all general meetings, regattas, etc." The reason for its non-enforcement may lie in the further clauses, which state that "the uniform shall be a blue coat with turn-over collar, club buttons, and skirts lined with white silk;

R.N.Y.C. REGATTA, 1906; ROTHESAY BAY

Yachts "Rosemary," "Vagrant" and "Tigris"

flaps or skirts with three buttons under, and one at skirt pockets; white or pale buff vests; blue or white trousers according to the season; black stock; blue cloth cap with gold lace band."

There is also gone the cruising in squadron formation, and the evolutions directed by signal from the Commodore which were once the chief part of the sport. It was when the racing interest came in that these fell off, and there are reasons for a suspicion that the modern Commodores were at times not above poking fun, themselves, at their own exalted position. It is told of one of them that leading the fleet down Channel with his stately old cutter, he was so intent upon the manœuvres he was directing that his own vessel ran hard and fast on the sands at Lamlash. The halyards were instantly cleared for a general order to the Fleet, and when the captains and owners spelled it out they read "Follow Commodore."

That spirit of exclusiveness which flourished so long in the navy was imitated also by the yacht club, and it was one of their rules that no vessel under eight tons burthen was eligible for ranking on the club books. The same spirit lingers still in the South, where the ownership of a vessel of at least thirty tons is made a condition for membership of the Royal Yacht Squadron. The rule, however, says nothing as to retaining the vessel after membership has been attained, and the result is that one cutter has been bought and sold by a long series of candidates in spite of a well-grounded doubt as to her ability to float if any of her numerous owners was rash enough to put her into the water. On the Clyde, however, the taste for day boats and bantam racers developed early, and the result was that in 1856 the Clyde Model Yacht Club—since become the Royal Clyde Yacht Club—was formed as a club exclusively for the owners of yachts which, because of their small size, were not eligible for membership of the older organisation. The headquarters and clubhouse of the Royal Northern Club are at Rothesay, and the Royal Clyde choose the higher stretches of the Firth, setting up house at Hunter's Quay. Their first clubhouse was burned, but they built again, and the present house, perched on a commanding position at the corner where the Holy Loch merges into the Firth, makes a prominent feature in the landscape.

After these there came in succession the Royal Western Yacht Club, now unfortunately on the wane, the enterprising Royal Largs, the Clyde Corinthian, for the special purpose of encouraging amateur sailing, the Mudhook, with its strictly limited membership, the Gourock Yacht Club, handsomely housed in a building presented to it by Mr. James Coats, junr., and the Holy Loch Club, which stands at the head of a long list of organisations encouraging racing in the more local form.

It is not the racing side of the pastime alone which is cultivated by these clubs, however. Soon after steam was introduced to the ships of the navy, and the mercantile marine, there was a move by a few of the bolder spirits to experiment with a power which seemed

R.N.Y.C. REGATTA, 1906

Yachts "White Heather," "Kariad," and "Nyria" jockeying for a start (Loch Striven in background)

to promise all the pleasure afloat with a minimum of that uncertainty which came of dependence on the errant breezes for motive power. The path of those reformers was not devoid of difficulties. Some of the older and influential clubs stood aghast at the desecration involved in the introduction of steam engines into the pastime, and the Royal Yacht Squadron in particular regarded the proposal with such antagonism that it passed a solemn decree of excommunication against any of its members who might dare to build or buy a vessel to be propelled by steam.

The Clyde was to the fore, however, in the development of the marine steamer, and with a number of eminent shipbuilders as enthusiastic supporters and sharers in the pastime it was but natural that the prejudice should be earliest and most successfully attacked in this district. Steam yachts soon made their appearance, doing in some respects more than the pioneers claimed for them and doing less in others. Of their continually increasing popularity there was, however, never any doubt, and the money that has flowed into the Clyde district for the building of steam yachts within the last half century represents an important phase of what is probably one of the greatest industries the world has ever seen. To the late Mr. George L. Watson more than to any other man the prosperity of this department of our shipbuilding is due. Now there are Watson steam yachts—easily recognisable by any with the most cursory knowledge of naval architecture—in every sea of the world, and the reputation they have achieved is flattering equally to the genius of the designer and the honest, skilful workmanship with which they were put together. The importance of the financial side of the industry may be estimated from the fact that one pair of vessels built side by side for two members of the Gould family represented an outlay of nearly half a million sterling.

In the matter of finance and in one or two other connections, the steam wing might claim to be the most important section of the pleasure fleet, and the argument might be the more readily admitted when it is acknowledged, as it must be, that it is from the sailing craft, and the racers in particular, that our yachting history gets its most interesting pages. A glance backwards over the events which linger in the memory of men still in active touch with the sport distinguishes a host of names of ships and owners, each of which carries its own cycle of interesting reminiscence, among them the *Vanduara*, the most famous of racing cutters, with the possible exception of the royal racer, *Britannia*; the little *Madge*, which, on the orders of her owner, Mr. James Coats, junr., and under command of that famous yachtsman of the old school, Captain Robert Duncan, went to America and swept the board there, stopping only outside the America Cup race because her tonnage was not sufficient to qualify her; and the *Wendur*, another famous vessel of the same date which in 1885 raced over the 33-knot course from Hunter's Quay to Blackfarland in 2 hours 17 minutes 28 seconds, and established a record which stood for seventeen years, until Mr. Peter Donaldson's *Bona*, driven to the limit by Captain Archie Hogarth, lowered the record to 1 hour 53 minutes 57 seconds.

Or if the tale of stirring matches be wanted, there is a wealth of them clamouring for attention. There is the Ailsa Craig match of 1885, when *Wendur*, *Galatea*, *Vanduara*, *Irex*, *Marjorie*, *Amandine* and *Tara* —famous racers all of them—gathered for the start. A southerly gale sprung up overnight, and in the morning there were only *Marjorie* and *Wendur*, with treble-reefed mainsails and spitfire jibs, ready to face the turmoil. They threshed it out with canvas often awash and spray flying over the racing flags which beat themselves to ribbons at the head of the housed topmasts, and *Marjorie* drew away ahead. But the troubles were not yet over. A slacking of the wind brought a fog of midnight darkness on the waters, and the steam yacht *Hebe*, which had been in attendance, ran hard and fast on the Ayrshire coast. *Marjorie* had bare time to haul out for safety, but the *Wendur*, following, mistook the lights of the stranded steamer for those of the fishing village of Portincross, and went also hard aground in an exposed and dangerous position, from which she was saved next morning comparatively uninjured. Nor is it possible to pass without reference to the important part which Clyde yachting men, owners, builders, and designers have played in the America Cup contest, a struggle which has lasted intermittently for over fifty years, and, yachtsmen say, will be continued until that much coveted trophy is brought back to this side of the Atlantic. The Clyde Syndicate *Thistle*, Lord Dunraven's three *Valkyries*, and Sir Thomas Lipton's three *Shamrocks* were all unsuccessful efforts towards this end, and there is still a hope that a Clyde cutter will break in upon our long-continued series of defeats.

CHAPTER XVIII

THE COWAL SHORE

Looking, on a winter night, from Gourock, Levanne, or the Cloch, across the Firth to the further hills, whose masses are indicated in the darkness only by the break of their silhouettes among the thickly-sprinkled stars, you realise, as you scarcely can by daylight, some of the sentiment that the Lowlands, where you stand, must have felt of old, fronting that barrier of cold, sounding sea which cut them off from the mystery and danger of the Highland world. In such an hour, on such a night, the tamed and trousered Scots pedestrian, making his way by the path along the Renfrew shore, must have sometimes felt himself on the very edge of civilisation, comfort, and peace, and his fancy must have then invested that looming mountain land with all the dreads and the forebodings then associated with wild and natural scenes, whose beauty was not yet discovered, and from which came frequent narratives of tribal war, pillage, fire, and massacre; and, more poignant still, that ghostly atmosphere of a bypast age and people, that dwells in

Gaelic speech and song and story. It is true that the east of the Firth was Gaelic itself to some extent, but its reformation came to it long before it came to Cowal; the Firth fulfilled for a later age that function of fence that at an earlier period had been performed a little to the south and east by the Roman Wall of Antoninus; and so sharp was the contrast between the peoples it divided, that while the citizens of Greenock busied themselves with legal barter and base mechanicals, the Campbells were massacring the Lamonts at Dunoon, the Atholemen were harrying the Campbells on the shores of the Holy Loch, and the forays of Rob Roy were carried to their very doors.

All communication with the sombre country of useless hills and sodden pathless valleys known as Cowal was by ferry from that point of land which to-day we call the Cloch. But who ferried to Dunoon from the douce shire of Renfrew, and all the unclanned industrious country at its back? Sometimes a king or queen, a chieftain home-returning, an invalid to drink goat's whey, or an adventurous merchant like Bailie Nicol Jarvie—there was little to tempt any others. Nor could there even be a traffic south in cattle; for that the peninsular character of Cowal was inconvenient, for all the droves for Lowland trysts and markets took roads far to the north by Glen Croe and Glen Falloch, and the Cloch at its best must have shown no wonderful animation, as did the marvellous fords between Benbecula and the Uists, or Stirling Bridge, or the pass at Arrochar. The charter for the right of

GLEN CROE

ferry to the Cloch was granted in 1658 by Archibald, Marquis of Argyll, to the Campbells of Ballochyle, on condition that they should have an eight-oared galley ready at any moment to convey his Lordship to the Renfrew shore. Its rights extended from the head of Holy Loch to beyond Dunoon, a distance of five or six miles; these rights were sold by the Ballochyles in 1825, to Hunter of Hafton, for two or three thousand pounds, and now they yield an infinitely larger sum per annum from the numerous piers along the shore. In that statistic fact is indicated the change that has come on Cowal in less than a hundred years.

If the change came to Cowal late, it came quickly, and the curious difference of aspect that is presented at night by both sides of the Firth between Innellan and Ashton bears closely and vitally upon that old vexed problem, the ownership of land. All along the Cowal shore the evening lamps make one continuous string of gems, that are not the least of the charms of Cowal for the dweller on the Renfrew side; but the Renfrew shore itself, from Wemyss Bay to Ashton, lies utterly dark, save for two or three far separate mansions, and the winking of the lighthouse at the Cloch. Why should it be so? Why should the Highland side of the Firth, a century ago so seemingly remote and uninviting, have become the health resort and playground of a teeming city—a fringe of villas, gardens, and prosperous towns, while the Renfrew side, so obviously better suited for such development, must still remain untenanted? It is no mere vain imagining to suggest that the contrast wholly rests upon the difference between the Highland and Lowland laird in character and fortune. From almost every point of view the Cowal shore is far inferior to the other side as a place of residence. Only two or three circumstances give it charms we cannot find across the Firth. It delights in the morning sun, while Gourock and Ashton still lie in shadow; it sees the glory of the early evening moonlight on the water, which for us is wholly lost; it has behind it the precious, romantic glens; its roads lead round or to the loveliest lochs in Scotland; and—what counts for much with me—it is Highland and Argyll.

But Cowal looks over to a country-side lacking all its own majesty of hill and glen and loch; it shivers in east wind, while Ashton snugly shelters in the lee of the Tower Hill and the high moor country; and it misses the magic colour that the forenoon throws upon the brake and heather, and the sunset lends to the flying cloud. Whom it was who first said the most beautiful walk in Scotland was from Gourock to the Cloch, and the next best from the Cloch to Gourock, will probably never be decided, though the saying is sometimes fathered upon the late Principal Caird; but the opinion was pious, and it could be much more truthfully applied to the Renfrew shore than to any part of the other side of the Firth. Not the mystery of the further hills by night, and the festival light of lamps on the other shore alone are ours; we see by day the deep indent of the blue sea-arms, the valleys opening and alluring that lead to places that we know where we were happy, that lead to loneliness and our fathers' wilds, and the lime-washed cot, and the singing river, and the rest of the evening inn. We see the mountain peaks sun-flecked, and covered by cloud and mist or shadow, varying in colour every hour; we see them austere and glittering under winter snows. And in certain blessed evenings, when the sun goes down behind Kilmun, and the Cowal people sit in unhallowed dusk, we see, over them, celestial glories, vistas of crimson and gold.

Why, then, should the Renfrew shore be dark and dwellingless, all save the crowded Gourock and Ashton terraces, that end, to the west, abruptly, just where the outlook is most excellent? It is so because Lowland Shaw-Stewarts have been more tenacious of their land, and more singularly fortunate than the Highland Campbell landlords on the Cowal shore. The amenities of Ardgowan are preserved by maintaining a desolate shore from Ashton to Wemyss Bay, and the owner of Ardgowan is sole owner of the shore in question, as he also is of Greenock. On the other side of the Firth the conditions for a hundred years have been very different. Less than a century and a quarter ago the whole of Cowal, from Lochgoilhead to Loch Striven, as far as Knockdow, was in the exclusive possession of Campbell lairds. Glenfinnart and Ardentinny were held by the Campbells of Ardkinglas and Ardentinny; Blairmore, Kilmun, Ardenadam, and farms on the river Echaig, by the Campbells of Monzie; Hafton and Orchard by the Campbells of

Orchard and Glendarvel; Benmore (formerly called Innis-nan-ruisg), Garrochoran, Dalinlongart, Dunloskin, and Dunoon Ferry, by the Campbells of Ballochyle; and Castle Toward Estate, by the Campbells of Auchawilling. Within the last 120 years all these very extensive lands have passed into the hands of Lowland proprietors, and there is not, I think, a single Campbell landlord of the soil left, except M'Ivor Campbell of Ballochyle. Three years ago I met him in Vancouver, British Columbia, a young and typical representative of the Scottish gentleman pioneer, exiled I hope not forever from the few acres left by Echaig; and one of the curious facts he told me was, that from the windows of Ballochyle House, at the head of Holy Loch, on a clear day, could be seen the chimney of St. Rollox, Glasgow.

Seventy years ago there was hardly a feu on Cowal. The first that was granted is said to have been the Argyll Inn at Sandbank, granted by Colonel Alexander Campbell of Ballochyle. In 1822 Dunoon was a Highland clachan, with a church, a manse, three or four slated cottages, and a sprinkling of thatched huts. Its first feu there was bought by Dr. James Ewing. A survey map of the Ballochyle estate, executed in 1819, which takes in the whole shore from Strone Point, by Kilmun, round the Holy Loch, on to Dunoon pier, a distance of seven or eight miles, shows less than a score of buildings—old Kilmun Church, old Kilmun Inn, the ancient Monastery Tower, old Kilmun House, two or three thatched cottages on the Kilmun side, and

DUNOON

the old school-house of Kilmun; the Argyll Inn, Sandbank, the Lazaretto or quarantine station for the Clyde; Orchard Park (now Hafton House), Dunoon Manse, Dunoon Inn, and a few small houses connected with the Dunoon Ferry. To-day how different; to-night how bright and habitable and cheerful with household fires look the long miles of the Cowal shore!

CHAPTER XIX

DOWN THE WATER—SUMMER

It was our grandfathers who found out what joys the Firth could hold for a holiday spirit—our grandfathers who worked till all hours in Glasgow shops, assured that that was life, and compelled to make the most of an annual week of playtime. Once they used to walk to Govan where the eggs were fresh and salmon was not expensive, and they thought a casual picnic there on the grass was as much of nature's rapture as mortal man need look for. Their noisier and more common pleasure took the form of "high jinks" round the booths, "geggies" and taverns of Glasgow Fair, and anywhere west of Kelvin was the wilds, to which one never went from the cosy city unless his health was poorly or his bills were to collect.

When Henry Bell had the *Comet* built for him in 1812, and she gallantly stood away to Helensburgh with a square-sail on her funnel, she was an oddity that might make us laugh to-day, but none-the-less she was a mighty portent, and not the least of her influences was the change she was to bring on Glasgow's notion of a holiday. She had the key to the hills and glens; she had the secret of the lochs and our now beloved western Archipelago. Behind her, still unrealised, merely draughts as it were in the drawing shops of Destiny, steamed a noble fleet of pleasure vessels bearing the city's millions to the shores that have become their playground. Govan, Camlachie and Stra'ven were to satisfy the roving cit no longer; he was into the age of Saturday-to-Monday travelling-bags and hazardous delights with rowing-boats at sixpence an hour. As Glasgow's vigour largely came from the West, either as food or men from the neighbouring Highlands, to the West she has ever looked with a wistful holiday eye, too much grime and a different people being to the east of her; so the Firth continues her especial Paradise. She cannot get there too often or too fast. Our grandfathers went by fly-boats—that must have got the name on the principle of *lucus a non lucendo*, since they took twelve hours to go from Broomielaw to Greenock under the most favourable circumstances; we could reach it now by paddle in less than two if we did not prefer the train to Gourock or Wemyss Bay, where we smell sea-wrack and hear the tide on the beaches forty minutes after leaving Glasgow.

It is perhaps the stranger's only fault with the Firth of Clyde that Glasgow has too palpably usurped it. He finds the shores interminably fringed by villas that have "suburb" written large on every feature from the name-plate and the aurucaria in front to the outhouse in the rear to which the owners retire when their home is let in the season. Such of these seaside dwellings as are not hired by the month by Glasgow families are the property of Glasgow men, their country houses; the Firth would have a poor existence wanting the approval and patronage of the city, thirty, forty, or fifty miles away. The month of May has no sooner lit the hills at night with fires of burning heather, brought the daffodil to the city parks, and made the terrors of the coming Whitsun term loom over the merchant's pillow like a nightmare than he yearns to escape to a place where he may briefly forget and sleep. Straightway his coast house—elsewhere in the East we should call it bungalow—is aired and opened, his wife and family—if the latter are not at school—go down to the sea, and he becomes a daily traveller. From Kilcreggan, Dunoon, Lochgoil, Rothesay, Millport, Largs, Arran, or the Kyles, he rises to a hurried breakfast, dashes to the quay to reach his city shop or office about nine o'clock, feeling like one who for a pearl quits the sunshine and the bounteous air to dive breathless in unpleasant and murky deeps. In the early evening he returns laden monstrously with groceries, or garden tools, or a pile of books from the Western Library. The natives know him as a man whose name is often in the newspapers, a pillar of the Second City; for four or five months he dwells among them, sharing humbly their interest in the signs of weather and the local kirk affairs, but they vaguely feel some sense of transiency in his presence; though

COLINTRAIVE, KYLES OF BUTE

with them he is not of them, even on the golf course; he is unmistakeably and hopelessly "a Gleska man."

Possibly he may not for more than a few weeks in mid-summer be able to quit the desk or counter save from Saturday-to-Monday; then his dull brown business hours are shot with moments of sunny dream, the thoughts of the coming holiday when town may be absolutely forgotten and the hard hat of a blameless life in commerce may be discarded for a cap or Panama. There is probably no other city in the world where such brief interregnums in a life of toil among the middle-classes are more universally the custom or more wholesomely utilised. It is the knowledge of the Firth at our back door, as it were, and of the happiness it proffers that makes Glasgow, for all its disabilities, a pleasant enough place wherein to strive for fortune.

But not to the upper and middle-class alone is the Firth of Clyde a sample of Paradise; there is no working-man, milliner, or seamstress in the city, who does not keep some dreams of happy days along its shores. Once a year Glasgow, tired, insurgent against toil, throws off her chains, damps down her furnaces, and hies her to the sea. It is her Fair. And over all the Firth there settles down in mid-July a swarm of citizens. In these days Glasgow's pall of smoke rolls back, and one may, from her eminences, see her from end to end, and the bastions of her protecting hills; the air alters and grows clean; a curious silence falls on streets for ordinary loud with footsteps and beseeching cries. The tide of life has ebbed and beats upon the distant estuary. Let us go to the Broomielaw in that too brief season and we shall find the quays packed dreadfully with people for the steamers which will take them down the river for a shilling; let us go by train to Greenock, Gourock, or Wemyss Bay, and we find ourselves swept onward still in the rush of holiday-makers bound for the favourite coast resorts yet further down. To sail in a Clyde passenger steamer at this time is so cheap a joy—it is cheap indeed at any season—that the national thrift compels us not to stay at home. In that one week in July, the Clyde coast towns, it must be owned, are no places for the contemplative pilgrim, the sensitive poetic soul. The great god Pan himself must take affright and skulk in the hill ravines; dryad and nymph must flee for a space to other scenes before the onset of St. Mungo's children, who come as an army with banners, to command the erstwhile quiet little towns, to bring the perfumes of the Trongate to the esplanades, to render lanes and fields and country roads untenable by their numbers and their pranks, to affront the moon with their uncouth gambols and the strains of their melodeons. There is no escape from them. The Glasgow accent—peculiar, indescribable, part Scots part Irish, to the stranger wholly unmusical—everywhere prevails; the Glasgow sportsmen stalk the whelk and cockle or cull edible sea-weeds on all the more insanitary beaches, or row with incredible lack of skill in small boats round the bays, a source of constant horror to the captains of the hurrying steamboats.

Down the Water—Summer

Who can grudge these children of the streets their week of manumission by the purifying sea or on the hill-sides whence so many of them came originally to lose their simple rustic airs and acquire a dubious urban cleverness? If the Firth be theirs for a week in July, all Summer is for luckier folk. I have written too hastily, perhaps, of the interminable fringe of villas—in truth the term is applicable only to the Cowal shore, and even there the Villa sometimes has as much of dignity as on Bellagio. There are massive dwellings, not inelegant, with lawns, tennis-courts, great gardens, vineries—summer homes of men retired from business, or of merchant princes, who have moorings out in the bay, and, nodding at them, white steam yachts that you may see in Autumn on the Baltic, or in Norwegian fiords, or in winter in the blue of the Mediterranean. All round the sea-shore go roads of the finest character, not so much the prey of the motor car as they might be in England, in Bute and Arran almost wholly free from its insistent hoot, its dust and swooping menace. Behind are peaceful lonely little glens, backwaters of life in a hurrying age, woods, hill-slopes purple with heather, and the spacious moors.

It is significant of Glasgow's close association with the coast that the very names of the steamers that daily ply there are dear to her, and their achievements in the way of speed or cheap teas are topics of universal and abiding interest. It might be natural that the city should take pride in the vessels that start at morning from the Broomielaw and cant at evening there, having still about them some air of holiday and adventure among fairer scenes, so that home-sick Highlanders go down to the harbour and find pleasure in the sight of the *Columba* or the *Lord of the Isles*; but there are steamers which Glasgow sees only when she is on holiday, and these she knows and loves almost as well—those of the railway companies whose sailings start at the end of a train journey to Greenock, Gourock or Craigendoran. There is no pleasure fleet in the world that offers so much for so small a cost. We know the captains by their Christian names; when pursers defalcate and disappear, as pursers will at times despite their haughty splendour, we feel a personal sense of shame or grievance, since we had come to look on them as intimates like our own domestics, with the prospect of being more permanent in office. Should you hear the names of Scott's heroes and heroines, or of Scottish nobles, or of Scottish scenes in any West of Scotland conversation, be sure it is not of literature, Burke's Peerage, or actual strath or glen the folk are speaking, but of some favourite river steamer, for the nomenclature of the fleet has always run in settled national lines.

If the Glasgow citizen in summer cannot spare the time for a more protracted outing on the Firth, he will go on an evening cruise after business hours, and he may even venture down the water on a Sunday, though there he gets small encouragement, either from popular sentiment or from railway or steamboat companies. A certain obloquy hangs about the "Sunday

TOWARD LIGHT

breakers," as the Sunday boats are called, and there are at present only two, which conduct their traffic on teetotal principles and on lines more decorous than their predecessors of some generations ago, for the Sunday breaker is no modern innovation, having often tried and failed. When the present Summer Sunday service was established a few years ago, Dunoon, remembering and alarmed at the prospect of rowdy Sabbaths, bolted the gates of her pier and refused the passengers admittance, but wiser counsels now prevail, and so far as can be seen, Dunoon at least is none the worse.

To be "down the water" on the Clyde in recent years was mightily different from being at an English watering-place—a Blackpool or a Margate. Great sandy beaches are unknown there; the shores descend too rocky and precipitate to retain any surface less than shingle; we gain by better drainage, but we lack a feature that the stranger, thinking of other coasts, might naturally expect. To bask or bathe from rocks, to fish and boat in the bays, were the only recreations of a purely marine character we could, till lately, offer. Now, places like Gourock, Dunoon, and Rothesay, pride themselves on their esplanades, where the pierrot, the minstrel, and the band have come to give our coast in the season something of an English aspect which may please the young but rouses mingled feelings in the middle-aged and elderly who remember more natural, less giddy times.

CHAPTER XX

WINTER ON THE FIRTH

The time to see the Firth most profitably, if it is not simply a sunburned face you want, but an exaltation of the mind, is not in summer, but in winter, when the black squall flies. It is good at all times—except when fogs possess it—but in January are charms unknown to travel there in July. There are, for instance, no bands upon the steamers, Hackenschmidts and Madralis of cornopian and concertina wrestling with Scotch airs that come badly mauled through the encounter, and you may venture into a saloon without the risk of finding little Maudie there before you playing the first part of the latest pantomime air on the public piano. I delight in the winter steamer to go down into the fore saloon as dusk comes on, and see the glowing stove with dusky forms about it, and hear men talk in the accents of Ardrishaig about hoggs and herrings, or catch the timid whisperings of the girl going south to her first situation. I like to mix with unaffected, healthy-looking fellow-creatures wearing top-boots and leggings—not in an ornamental affectation, as the young city man does in summer in a pathetic attempt thus to "get back to nature," and look very fit and rural, but because top-boots and leggings are essential to their business. I like to stand in the warm lee of the funnels, with men covered up in oil-skins, and other men with thick, inartistic-coloured blunt-cut clothes and squashy hats—farmers and the like—not "redolent of R. L. S.," as a lady once said to me of Edinburgh, but mildly of sheep-dip, whisky, and plug tobacco, and hear the wind whistle in the cordage, and see through the blurr of rain the winking of the lights of Toward, Cloch, and the Gantocks. Then there is something compact, friendly, communal, about a Clyde steamer; the very purser, no longer gold braid from clew to earing, as the sailor says, but human, wet, and unaffected, as oil-skin clad he bears a hand at a rope; the captain so much on a plane with all of us that we feel we may, without offence, call him Duncan and be done with it. A Clyde steamer in July is like a section of Sauchiehall Street cut out and sharpened at each end, with engines in the middle to go down and look at; but at this time of the year it is pure Highland, a thing apart, as dignified as a mountain, and as full of real "characters" as a clachan.

We leave Gourock, say, this winter day, in a south-west gale, in the *Duchess of Montrose*, her saloon windows shuttered against the seas, and make for the mouth of the Holy Loch. I never cared much for the Holy Loch; its mud and shingle come too quickly, so I am glad we are not going in there.

Hunter's Quay receives us, and here you have the first idea of winter days at the coast. A deserted pier, but for two men in oil-skins to catch the ropes; paraffin oil casks piled against the railings; flag-pole halyards flap-flapping in the winds; villas, sombre and black with rain, standing in gardens of glistening shrubbery; thin brown woods behind the village; in front a rain fog hiding the other side of the Firth. Not much doing at Hunter's Quay. A man with a brown-paper parcel gets off the steamer reluctantly, his coat-collar high on his ears, and bending to the wind, stands a moment to watch the ropes cast off, and looks after the steamer as she proceeds on her way. He is sorry he came. Any other day might have done, perhaps. He looks over his shoulder at the village, and once more at the wake of the steamer, and then he slowly goes up the pier. At Kirn, where we stop next, the red tiles and gilt of the waiting-room suggest that somebody has got a part of the old Glasgow Exhibition down for wintering—a piece of frivolity belated, and quite out of keeping with its surroundings. More paraffin oil casks in profusion—plainly the chief import of the coast town at this season is paraffin oil. Not much doing at Kirn either. A gentleman with a tall silk hat comes on board. He has evidently eluded the vigilance of the local hotels, and made his escape, for when the steamer resumes her way he stands beside the paddle-box, his silk hat—which looks as appropriate to the situation and the season as a Spanish mantilla would do—clutched firmly by both hands, and throws a look of relief upon Kirn as the rain-blur wipes it out behind us.

And then Dunoon. Where is Winnie? or Marion? or Agnes? or whatever her name was, who, with her comrades, stood so persistently on this pier in August, and waved studiously graceful adieux after her friends bound for the city? On that spray-swept wharf there ought to be the wraith of the Summer Girl in muslin and chiffon, the Tam o' Shanter on her glorious head, the walking-stick in her hand, the happy consciousness in her heart that, even if the wind does blow, her shoes are of the neatest. Summer Girl! Summer Girl! In wintry gales to-day I think of you, so dainty and so sweet, the fairest flower of the summer gardens, so fresh, so tanned, so rosy with the wholesome air of the sea. I loved you, Summer Girl; I loved you, one and all; many a time we walked and talked together, but you never knew it, 'twas but an old man's ghost! To-day not even your wraith haunts the pier of Dunoon. My heart will not go out to Highland Mary on her pedestal. I never liked her—there; but much less loveable than usual does Highland Mary look in the drenching rain, wind buffeted. She is no ethereal spirit of the hills; her very existence there shows that in Scotland we do not understand. The poet's Mary was a Mary of the mind—the winds of spring were her breathing; her voice was the sound of water in tiny glens; her eyes were the remote and unfathomable stars. She died—it was always so; he never married her—and so it was bound to be, that a memory and unattainable, she should rise for ever before him, the virgin bride of fancy. Little doing in Dunoon, only a clammy, inefficient statue of a dream. And a policeman, monstrous in his cape. More casks of paraffin, too; bathing places deserted, gardens sodden, rows of villas silent and dead, hills behind menacing. No; we will not go ashore at Dunoon. Into the teeth of a stiffer wind we proceed towards Innellan, to see the Bullwood houses snuggling in their hollows, to speculate upon what is at the other end of the gaps of glens in the hillsides, to discover the burns roaring down in hundred-feet falls, and snow-white.

At Innellan more paraffin oil and a yellow dog; a woman struggling with an umbrella blown outside in; but positively nothing doing except the landing of some groceries and weekly papers. Before us lies Toward, that in this grey gale might be the end of everything, for beyond the point is nothing visible. Through the steamer goes the wrenching sound of struggle; the engines pant and heave distressed in the midst of her, wild gusts blow in alley-ways, tarpaulins flap, the funnel whoops with wind. We cannot make Craigmore, but land at Rothesay. One solitary badge porter—last of all his tribe—stands on the pier and points his finger at us. Do we look like folk that come with baggage to stay at the "Madeira" in days like these? 'faith, no, we have homes! But in truth Rothesay always seems to me a more habitable and desirable place in winter than when Wull the Glasgow larrikin possesses the pier, and the minstrels are on the

LOCH FYNE

esplanade. It is the ideal size of a winter town—big enough for warmth, and a sort of self-contained society, not big enough to catch the music-hall disease or to have an unpleasant number of strangers coming about. It seems to shrink in the rain; its sea front to be only half as long as when Glasgow crowds the pavements and the esplanade; the hotels have lost a good deal of their importance with the taking down of their flags. We walk a lonely road to Ascog, in front of which the sea is white with spindrift; but this is too like going into the wilds, and we return hastily to Rothesay, and its shops, and its tramway cars, that look as real as anything, and run with frequency, as if in weather like this there were actually people who wanted to get to Port-Bannatyne.

Before we are half-way back to the mainland the night is almost come. It is then that a one-and-nine-penny trip in a river steamer has the faint suggestion of adventure double the money cannot buy when you go in summer sunshine by the *Columba*, the *Lord of the Isles*, or the turbines. Night, and a gale, and flying spray, and the ship heaving; the land out of sight, and the red-hot stove in the saloon, and slightly odorous paraffin lamps swinging responsive to the roll of the waves; a smell of brine and tarpaulin, a thumping of doors, a clanging of shovels down below, the muffled tread of sea-boots, and the flap of oil-skins. No band, no Maudie at the piano, no excursion party at the bows singing "Rolling Home to Bonnie Scotland," no sense of holiday, but a feeling that everybody is here on the business of his life. Far before us a star shines on a dim promontory for a moment, and then dies out, to be revealed again and again. It is the light of the Cloch, and closer, but less ardent-white, begins to wink the light on the skerry called the Gantocks.

DUNDERAVE CASTLE, HEAD OF LOCH FYNE

CHAPTER XXI

LOCH FYNE

Of the Clyde sea-arms, Loch Fyne, which now we come to, has doubtlessly figured most importantly in the earlier periods of Scottish history, though we must judge of that more by deduction than by surviving story. Its immensely greater expanse than that of the other lochs; its deeper penetration into the country; its situation and its natural resources gave it prior claims on the invader and the settler, and the early establishment near its head of a great feudal family, the Campbells, brought it more prominently into relation with the lowland world. It was the Mediterranean Sea of the Dalriadic Celts who came from Ireland; Magnus Barefoot knew its shores and coves, and claimed no small part of them for Norway by a stratagem of a character not uncommon among Celts and Scandinavians if all folk tales be true. The law ran, more or less limpingly, on Loch Fyneside, and a certain security of domestic peace was there while as yet Loch Long, Loch Lomond and the Gareloch were open to the excursions and alarms of petty clans and the depredations of gentlemen like Rob Roy.

With the greater part of Loch Fyneside for generations under the hand of the Argylls and their cadets, it had the position of an *imperium in imperio*, and prosperous internal states of the kind knit together by the ties of blood and common interest are not lightly to be meddled with by envious or resentful peoples outside the pale. Thus, singularly few attacks of any moment were made on the integrity of Loch Fyne, considering the temptations it must have offered; it was ill to get at with an adequate force of footmen, for the passes to it were hard to traverse and easy to guard, and there is no record of "spulzie" by ships. Montrose made its shores the objective of a demonstration in force by his lieutenant Colkitto in 1644, and the men of Athole, with hoardes of clansmen from further north, plundered both sides of it in 1685, but it was, save on these occasions, exempt from the more serious manifestations of Highland strife. Even Rob Roy, when he borrowed the potent name of Campbell and came to the head waters of the Shira to a cot whose ruins still look over Loch Fyne, had to comport himself like an honest man.

Whether the "guile of the Campbells" differed in anything more than degree from the guile of any other powerful family of the feudal days it would ill become a tenant of the Campbells to expatiate on, but at least the clan's diplomacy always led to

INVERARAY

desirable results in civilization even if the methods might have been open to criticism. The old Dalriada or Earaghaidheal was early in the seventeenth century a tolerable enough place for lowland merchants and mechanics to settle in, secure of Argyll's protection, and up till 1745 the good government of the greater part of the Highlands, the restraint of the Jacobite clans particularly, depended upon that portion of Clan Campbell territory that borders Loch Fyne and has its focus in the now declining and somnolent Royal Burgh of Inveraray. It was to the Duke of Argyll—the MacCailen Mor—and his vassals the government of the eighteenth century looked for the proper subjection of his turbulent neighbours on the west—the Stewarts, Camerons, Macdonalds and others of the old regime. According to an official report submitted to the government in 1750 the Duke and his clan, including Breadalbane, could raise if necessary 10,000 men able to bear arms. The bulk of them must have been found between the shores of Loch Fyne and Loch Awe: single glens of Loch Fyne could turn out over two hundred swords; now they are desolate, though there were none of the wholesale clearances that dispeopled many other parts of the Highlands.

It is, however, in a purely commercial connection that Loch Fyne is known to our day—as the source of a surprisingly succulent variety of herring. Its fame for herring is hundreds of years old; Frenchmen used to barter wine for herring at a point called

Rudha nan Fraingeach, a few miles out of Inveraray, and many generations of Loch Fyneside men have followed a vocation which has much of the uncertainty of backing horses without so much amusement. Towns like Inveraray, Lochgilphead, and Tarbert grew up, as it were, round the fishing smacks that in old days ran into their bays for shelter, and Minard, Crarae, Lochgair, Castle Lachlan, Strachur, and other villages on either side of the loch depend to some extent for their existence on the silver harvest of the sea. A fish whose migratory movements still baffle the scientist, the herring is elusive and erratic, and seasons of success are divided by recurring periods when the shoals appear to go elsewhere. The means of capture are netting, either with the drift net kept on or near the surface by buoys and stretched out to great lengths to intercept the shoals, or with the seine net, here called the "trawl," in which two skiffs combine to run a net round the shoal or "eye" of fish wherever it is observed. Sailing up Loch Fyne in daytime when the fishing skiffs are in the harbours, the loch vacant of active life, it is difficult to conceive that the same great empty stretch of water may at midnight be busy with hundreds of boats, when the cry of the fishers as they "hale" their nets, the lights of their flares as they summon the steamers to carry their takes to the Clyde, give the mid-channel all the aspect of a town.

The loch is about forty miles long and one to

TARBERT, LOCH FYNE

five miles broad, with its portals opening at Skipness and Ardlamont; hills enfold it, that, except at the head, have not the same sublimity as those of Arran looming near the entrance. The Knapdale hills on the left indeed are tame; the Cowal hills on the other shore are suave in parts to monotony. Only in the upper reaches is there any multitude of trees; there the Argyll estate is clothed with ancient forest, which Dr. Johnson must have gone through with his eyes shut. But some reclusive charm is in these hills and bays that is not elsewhere; you have left the changing lowland world behind you at Ardlamont, and breathe a more romantic air. Tarbert, coyly hiding itself in a winding, lake-like inlet, fretted by rocky promontory and isle, is a fishing village, crouched at the feet of a ruined keep which Robert Bruce inhabited. Quarter of a century ago it was the St. Ives of the Scottish painter; to-day the taste for yellow wrack and fishing-skiffs is somewhat in abeyance, but the same spirit, pensive mystery, and expectation haunt the place as Colin Hunter found in his "Trawlers waiting for Darkness." It is only a narrow neck of land that keeps Loch Fyne from the appealing arms of the Atlantic. Magnus Barefoot, reading lawyer-wise the treaty by which King Malcolm of Scotland ceded all the islands "between which and the mainland he could pass in a vessel with its rudder shipped," landed at West Loch Tarbert, according to the Orkneyinga Saga, and had a boat drawn across the isthmus to Loch Fyne, himself holding the rudder, so that he secured for the Norse the whole of the Kintyre peninsula, "which is better than the best island of the Sudreyar, except Man." Hakon later in like wise evaded the rough, long passage round the Mull of Kintyre, and, forty years after Hakon, Robert the Bruce portaged it also, since which time a canal or shipway has been Tarbert's great ambition.

But the canal to the Atlantic is already made elsewhere—ten miles further up the loch, no great thing as canals go, though picturesque, fit only to float a tiny passenger steamer or a cutter yacht. Ardrishaig is its entrepot, at the mouth of Loch Gilp, at the head of which is a quiet and pleasant township, left at low tides to the rueful contemplation of an unattractive stretch of muddy shore. A curious sand spit and a group of rocks almost bar the passage up Loch Fyne at Otter; a little further north of them fishermen dry their nets, and surely fairies dwell in the green creek of Lochgair. Still further north, on the left, are the manorial lands of Minard, with a handsome modern castle, and the great whin quarries of Furnace and Crarae. The village of Strachur, on the right, is the terminus of the route which David Napier opened from Kilmun by Loch Eck; twenty minutes' sailing brings us to the county town of Inveraray, which stands on a promontory, under wooded hills, whose foliage renders more distant and austere the myriad peaks that culminate in Cruachan, by Loch Awe. Six miles further inland, Loch Fyne,

STRACHUR, FROM DALCHENNA, LOCH FYNE

having narrowed quickly from the point where stands the ruined sixteenth-century castle of the MacNaughtons of Dunderave, ends in the brackish pools of the river Fyne.

It is the north end of Loch Fyne that, till recent years, travellers have seen most of, since, before the coming of the steamer, the road by Arrochar, Glen Croe, and Inveraray was the highway from the lowlands to the west coast and the isles. This way came Faugas de Saint Fond in 1784, to find French spoken at the dinner table of Inveraray Castle "with as much purity as in the most polished circles of Paris"; this way came Robert Burns, to find the very antithesis of that "Highland welcome" he declared could not be bettered over Acheron; this way, too, came Keats to Inveraray to have his first experience of the bagpipe, as sole orchestra at a performance of Kotzebue's "Stranger" in the ducal barn. Dorothy Wordsworth and her brother had come the same road fifteen years before, and though Inveraray on a closer inspection scarce approved itself to the tidy dame, her first impression was that it looked as pretty as a raree show—"or pictures of foreign places—Venice, for example—painted on the scene of a play-house." Dr. Johnson and Boswell found in its inn, which remains unchanged, "as good a room and bed as at an English inn"; the Doctor called for a gill of whisky, to taste what "makes a Scotchman happy," and Bozzy drank the dregs of his idol's glass. Turner painted the bays, woods, and hills of the neighbourhood with an artistic ecstasy that soared above all considerations of topographical accuracy.

On a summer day, if you be fortunate, you may sail from end to end of Loch Fyne on a surface without a ripple, in a silence undisturbed save by the cry of birds. Flocks of divers scatter and sink before your bows, the porpoise wheels in the sunshine ; you may even see a whale roll out of Kilfinan Bay, leisurely chasing herring, lord of the fiord, huge, in love with himself and the heat of the day, and the sting of salt on his hide and the taste of fish. You may see the gannet fly, too, high in heaven, and plunge like an arrow from the height. The very cottages on the hill-sides are transfigured then, and seem more habitable than palaces. Even winter brings its own stern beauty to Loch Fyne, when the peaks of snow are mirrored on its surface, or the ice-floe roars at high tide on its beaches. The stones of Inveraray Castle were brought from the opposite side of the loch on sledges, and twenty-seven years ago skaters disported themselves, miles from its head, as on an artificial pond.

INVERARAY CASTLE
The seat of the Duke of Argyll

CHAPTER XXII

WIDER SHORES

"Strath Clutha, or the Beauties of the Clyde," is a characteristic product of the early nineteenth century when Books of Beauty, either in person or prospect, were part of the equipment of every drawing-room, and the art of the steel engraver, which has come to be too lightly esteemed, perhaps, was at its highest. I can never look at the engraved drawings of D. O. Hill without a certain feeling of dejection, as one who realises he has come at least half a century too late to see Scotland at its best. He made our landscapes as heavenly beautiful as Turner ever dreamt in Italy; eternal sunshine smiles on vales that have familiar names but are enveloped somehow in the atmosphere of Tempe; his ruins are the fresh-scrubbed petrified embodiment of old romance; his peasantry are short-kilted Watteau folk in a perpetual *fête champêtre*, under the noblest kinds of trees or by the sides of re markably well-omposed rivulets that purl. These illustrations must have often sadly misled credulous good people who accepted them as veritable transcripts of things seen, packed their bags in a hurry and came holidaying in a land so fair, in which clouds were always the fleecy or dappled kind, rain was merely a rare phenomenon always in the distance, and poverty and decay were always picturesque. I cannot believe that D. O. Hill and all the other artists and engravers of the period saw Scotland just like that: at least they did not see it "through a temperament" (which is Art, as the sage says), but only partly through their own eyes and mostly through the eyes of great painters who had dealt with classic scenery before. "Strath Clutha" is an elegant album of engravings by Joseph Swan, after drawings by himself and others, and it is in the most determinedly classic spirit of the age. The sea is invariably of a reflective calm which does not prevent the shipping from having canvas stiff with wind; the villas and castles gleam with marble whiteness in an unfailing sun; the towns are all Arcadian; the air is ever of a crystal quality that reveals the most infinite detail of the furthest hills. A certain charm emerges from these conventional illustrations; they are not Scotland as we know it ourselves, but they suggest the kind of Scotland we might have had if we better deserved it. One thing is plain from them, as from nearly all the engravings of the time, that the executants had not discovered the delight of truth to that vital element of the landscape—weather.

If in these chapters on the Clyde I have not said much about the weather it has been from no intention

CARRADALE PIER AND THE
CAMPBELTOWN BOAT

to gloss over what is notorious. They record for the most part but impressions, and in retrospect our days are always delightful, though they may have included tempest or rain. It is but fair to say, however, that to the stranger at least the weather is likely to be no trivial factor in his judgment of the Clyde, and it cannot be denied that there are more clouds and rain in our summer season than the old engravers even to themselves confessed. To the average atmosphere of our Spring, Summer, and Autumn, Mr. and Mrs. Hunter, in the drawings for this volume, have been strictly faithful, though they may have abated a storm or two. Our rainfall is typical of the west coast of most countries, heavy on the high ground, less so on the low ground, and everywhere showing a maximum in winter (December and January being the wet months of the year) and a minimum in early summer, the driest months as a rule being May and June. When it rains in midsummer it is apt to rain with a gusto that is not exhausted for days, and in such weather the charming views whose presentment is before the reader have a different complexion, sometimes no less dear to us who are familiar with it. It is with a shrewd commercial view of compensating their visitors for the eccentricities of the climate that the coast resorts depending most on crowds have in recent years not only greatly improved their roads and sea-fronts and beaches, but have discovered distractions to mitigate the depression of wet days. Dunoon, particularly, knowing that the most cheerful souls can take no great delight from the prolonged contemplation of "Highland Mary's" statue dripping on the skirts of the hill on which stood the ancient castle of the Scottish Lord High Stewards, has lately opened a commodious and artistic pavilion, which, for concert purposes, gives a wet day alternative to the public gardens surrounding it. The capital of Cowal, accordingly, prospers by the more faithful patronage of visitors who might otherwise be attracted to the competing gaieties of Ireland and the Isle of Man, whose dancing halls have not, luckily, been made a feature of the Clyde.

The other Clyde resorts—Rothesay excepted—are content to depend on the graces of nature to bring them the essential public, save in a few instances where the "sand-busking" minstrel breaks in discordantly on the music of wind and wave, and expects a public contribution to his shell. Whoever would avoid these features of modern European life at the coast, and choose a more reclusive air, is safe to go to any of the little hamlets in the lochs or on the long coast line of peninsular Kintyre. Between Skipness, at the mouth of Loch Fyne, and Campbeltown there are thirty miles of sea-shore that gives at every part the most entrancing prospect of the firth and its islands. Skipness, Carradale, and Saddell, on Kilbrannan Sound, are the most obvious of the many alluring little creeks or bays that open from the rivulets descending from a vertebrae of hills neither steep, barren, nor rocky. Skipness in its castle has an imposing structure of high antiquity well preserved; Carradale, on its rocky headland, has another ruined stronghold of the island lords and a vitrified fort, crowning a small peninsula; Saddell, further south, has the ruins of a Cistercian abbey built by the Macdonalds, Lords of the Isles.

Old memories even more numerous are associated with Campbeltown, the capital of Kintyre, though its name is redolent of a spirit more modern that emanates from a score of whisky distilleries. The well sheltered bay of Campbeltown, at the head of a three-quarter mile long loch, sheltered by the natural mole created by the island of Davaar, had too obvious advantages to be resisted by the first of the Irish Scots who, not very greatly daring, crossed the thirteen miles of water that separate Kintyre from the north of Antrim, and made Kintyre the cradle of the Dalriadic kingdom. Nor could, we may be sure, the Lochlanners, the Strangers, black or fair, of the Scandinavian galleys, having breathlessly swung round the beetling headland of the Mull, fail to take advantage of the first friendly haven of the great strange fiord. It became, as Kilkerran, one of the cradles of Christianity in the west; the Macdonalds, Lords of the Isles, made it capital of their sea domain. Over the bleak plain behind it was the way to the Machrihanish, on whose sands the Atlantic burst. James V., failing to shatter the power of that arrogant intractable tribe, gave a grant of their territory to the Campbells of Argyll, with power to seize and hold by sword. Macdonalds and Campbells fought for many years, the district became a waste, but Argyll prevailed, and settled Kintyre by peaceful levies of lowlanders from the opposite mainland of Cunninghame, Carrick and Kyle. Kintyre, thus influenced by its lowland colonists, who still help to make it the richest possession of MacCailen Mor, has long had an Ayrshire touch in the character of its people. Their fathers came from the more fertile side of the firth—pious men of the Covenant, and good farmers.

The beauty of the Renfrewshire and Ayrshire shores in particular appealed to the artists of "Strath Clutha." For miles below the Cloch light they found stately mansions like Ardgowan, Kelly Castle, Skelmorlie, and Kelburne, distinguished by that air of exotic opulence they cherished in their drawings. Those houses "cock their beavers" still conspicuously on the plateaux round the eastern shore, but save at Ardgowan, which tolerates only the ancient village of Inverkip in its propinquity, and that in discreet background, they have been rudely jostled by the ambitious dwellings of modern sea-kings, like the Inverclydes of Castle Wemyss, of men of commerce like the late owner of Kelly Castle, or scientists like Lord Kelvin of Netherhall, or by the terraces whose red sandstone villas have an air that is so different from the prevalent grey masonry of other places. Wemyss Bay, Largs, Fairlie,—they are Glasgow's railway exits to the lower firth; if Hugh Macdonald

"BARKING" HERRING NETS, CARRADALE

saw them now he would not recognise them, they have changed so much in half a century. A hydropathic suns itself on the cliffs; Atlantic liners, new from the builders' hands, test their speed on a measured mile below—this is Skelmorlie, and the castle on the hill is the Earl of Eglinton's. Further down the coast Largs looks out round the upper end of the Great Cumbrae, with a kindlier welcome to the democracy. It is one of the most popular summer resorts on the coast. An aisle of the seventeenth century in the centre of the town, is the mausoleum of the Montgomeries, and the vault contains the dust of that gallant Sir Hugh, who took Hotspur prisoner on the field of Otterburn. On a plain to the south of Largs, called Haylee, Hakon of Norway fought his last fight for the Hebrides, and the house of Kelburne, Lord Glasgow's seat, in the woody embrasure of the hills beyond, is old enough in parts to have looked upon the conflict. Fairlie, below it, was, a century ago, a fishing village, and, till lately, difficult of access. Long noted for its boat-building, Fairlie has contributed for nearly a hundred years to the reputation of the Clyde for naval architecture. The Fifes built the steamboat *Industry* of 1814, and the boats designed and built by the Fifes of our own day, father and son, continue to command the admiration of all decerning yachtsmen. These are storied shores, from Portincross or Goldenberry to Girvan; ruins on the headlands hold a thousand memories of our troubled ancient days, though, in the crescent front of Kyle, Ardrossan, Saltcoats, Troon, and Prestwick busy themselves with golf or commerce, and the town of Ayr must this time vainly tempt to another chapter on the Land of Burns.

CHAPTER XXIII

THE ISLANDS

To the wider firth that lies between the coasts of Renfrew and Ayr and the peninsula of Kintyre the islands give a grandeur to which the most familiar intimacy never makes a Scotsman quite indifferent, and to which the stranger comes for the first time with surprise and fascination. Lacking the splintered peaks of Arran, the green headlands of Bute, and the rocky terraces of the Cumbraes, the Channel from the Cloch to Ailsa Craig might be more to the mind of a sailor beating down at night in dirty weather, but their impediment is rarely serious and their presence gladdens the eye that otherwise might weary of the long monotony of the far separate mainland shores. We search the British map in vain for such another happy entrance to commercial waters. Galway Bay alone has something remotely similar, but infinitely less noble and arresting to the eye, in the barren and melancholy Aran isles. It was for us, a happy hour of Nature's travail, when she severed the ligaments that bound the Cumbraes to the ruddy sandstone and trap of the shores of Ayr, sundered the north of Bute from the clay and mica of Cowal, and in one supreme convulsion heaved off the burden of the sea and raised the Arran granite thousands of feet in air. They gladden folks in ships, these islands, and they inestimably enrich the prospect for mainland people. How much the poorer would the westward outlook be from Ayrshire wanting the purple shadows in the glens of Arran, the trailing mists on its shoulders, and the sunfleck and the snow on its sierras.

Of the three island groups in the firth, Bute calls first for notice as the most familiar to the holiday hours of the west of Scotland, and as nearest to the mainland, from which it is separated by a strait so narrow that drovers used to make their cattle swim it in their traffic with the markets of Argyll. Indented by beautiful sandy bays, traversed by lovely valleys running east and west, with no high hills to impose their shadows and attract rain, Bute is distinguished by its expansive area of verdant foliage and sward. The mountains of Cowal fling fond arms round its head and comfort it against the northern winds ; its climate has been the chief cause of its prosperity ; flowers flourish there that will grow nowhere else in Scotland, and strawberries and roses are sometimes seen blossoming in midwinter. That portion of the island which is washed by the Kyles is unprofitably barren though beautiful ; the fruitful, habitable parts are the middle and lower ends below Kames and

ROTHESAY CASTLE

Ettrick Bays. Rothesay is there, snugly tucked in a bay that must have given much joy to its first discoverers, as it has to millions since. Behind, on the uplands, are three small lakes. Apart from the story of Rothesay and its castle there is little history to chronicle regarding Bute. Stone circles at Kingarth, near Kilchattan, and St. Colmac, close to Ettrick Bay, have their own suggestions, but preserve their inviolate secret for all but speculation. At Dungoil, near the north end of the island, is an old fused whinstone fort that doubtless belongs to an age earlier even than Dalriadic or Norse invasion; ruins of towers like Kilmorie, Kilspoke and Kames, and of chapels like St. Ninian's, St. Cormac's, and St. Blane's, and the old cathedral church of St. Mary are records of the mutability of tangible things of faith and fond possession.

Round Rothesay Castle which stands in silent pathos and ineptitude in the centre of a town that is the very spirit of modernity, old tides of battle beat for centuries. It is supposed to have been built by Magnus Barefoot in 1098. Surrendered to the Scots, the Norse recovered it, but were finally dispossessed of it by the Stewarts, and thereafter leaguer and loss and fire by a succession of contending people were its portion. Cromwell's troops destroyed it in 1650; a quarter of a century later it was burned by the Argylls. Stewart kings dwelt in it, and one of them died there, finding moated walls and stark portcullis no defence against the siege of sorrow that broke his heart. Rothesay town and the eager city throngs who have made it for years the most popular coast resort on the Clyde, too rarely pause, I fear, to meditate on all this. It is not for vagrant airs of old romance and humbling contemplation of the mighty fallen that the thousands flock summer after summer to this Margate of the North, with its great arc of esplanade, its congeries of hotels, boarding-houses and villas, its pierrots and its bands. They come for pleasure from more fleeting things, and modern Rothesay—with a jealous eye on its competitor Dunoon—does the best it can for them. They may add to pleasures purely urban, though found in the presence of the immemorial hills across the way, the more simple joys to be got in the beautiful bay that has inspired the muse of popular song, or on the lovely roads that circle and intersect the island over which the Marquess of Bute is lord.

To the south-east of Bute, separated from the Marquess's princely home, Mountstuart, by the main channel which the shipping follows, and from the mainland by a narrow sound, are the Great and Little Cumbraes, whose spiritual father in Millport prayed for them once, as the hackneyed story goes, with an added intercession for "the adjacent islands of Great Britain and Ireland." Millport and its sunny southern bay—which in stiff sou'-westers takes a mightily different complexion—are its principal features; no trace is left of the camp which Hakon formed on the eve of the battle of Largs. A mile and a half

CRAIGMORE AND ROTHESAY BAY

across the "Tan" is the lesser Cumbrae with a ruined sanctuary on its hill, a single farm, a lighthouse, and a strong old roofless tower on an islet, which Robert II. occupied, and Cromwell's troopers burned in an hour of pique or vengeance.

Keats, like many another commentator after him, expressed his surprise that Robert Burns, in Ayr, with the Arran hills so prominently before him, should apparently have got no fervour of poetry from their presence. The finest views of Arran are to be got from the Ayrshire shore, which sees the purple come upon leagues of heather, the clouds mantle the cavernous glens, and a fantastic forest of alpine peaks struck black against the dying light of the west. Burns, a landward man and a lowlander (however Celtic his descent), notoriously walked with a stooped shoulder; daisy, thistle, and "timorous beastie" did not escape his affectionate observation, but he got no lyric impulse from the mystery of cloud and glen and these stupendous mountains.

The island, which has an area of 165 square miles, is most densely mountainous towards the north, where summit after summit rises from the Cock to the finial of Goatfell, 2866 feet high. Goatfell soars on the east abruptly from the water level, and commands the eye by a majesty that is only a hundred feet or two more eminent than that of Ben Tarsuinn, Cir Mhor, and Caisteal Abhail, to which it is joined by ridge and spur behind. Mural cliffs and wild acclivities distinguish it on the north and west, where it starts from the engirdling glens of the Sannox and the Rosa: to the south it ascends more gradually from Brodick Bay, and from this side usually do climbers reach its eminence, which reveals a world of waters, glens, and mountains, from Mull to Ben Ledi, from Cruachan to the Irish coast. The southern half of the island consists of undulating plateau, tamer hills, and bleaker valleys; the sea, whose ancient level makes a terrace round the island, and forms its encircling road, doubtless once intersected it with little lochs; but Arran now has a singularly unbroken coast line, deeply indented only at Lamlash, Brodick, and Loch Ranza.

The "Monarina" of Ptolemy, the "Hersey" of the Norse, who held it till Somerlid took it from them, Arran has a sufficiency of history, authentic and fabulous, to tempt to the pedestrian style of the guide-book cicerone. Nevertheless its archaeological remains are far from numerous, considering its size and the place it has in the story of our country, and fearless enterprising men have eked them out by "discoveries" of the graves of Ossian, Fingal, Malvina, and Oscar. We stand with more emotion by the menhirs of Tormore, the ruins of Kildonan Keep, and old Loch Ranza Castle; they minister better to the imagination. On two occasions at least Arran was the sanctuary of Robert the Bruce, whose gratitude to its people found expression in grants of land to them when he got the crown. With one exception these heritages passed from the descendants of the men on whom they were

GLEN SANNOX, ISLE OF ARRAN

conferred; and almost the entire island—long held by the Dukes of Hamilton—now belongs to the daughter of the twelfth Duke, wife of the Marquis of Graham, who is heir to the dukedom of Montrose. Brodick Castle, under Goatfell, is their residence, the "big house" of the island, comparatively modern most of it, in spite of its craw-stepped gables, but some of its walls date from the time of Bruce, and on the site was originally a stronghold of the Norse. The little village in the sandy bay beside it, with three romantic glens behind, shares with Lamlash such tourist traffic as the island attracts. Lamlash, with the Holy Island as a breakwater for its commodious bay, which has sheltered Hakon's shattered fleet and the cruisers of King Edward with equal hospitality, is the business centre of the island. Loch Ranza, on the north coast, facing Kilbrannan Sound, backed by the loftiest mountains, haunted by fishing skiffs, has inspired a stanza in "The Lord of the Isles."

"On fair Loch Ranza streamed the early day.
Thin wreaths of cottage smoke are upward curled
From the lone hamlet which her inland bay
And circling mountains sever from the world.
And there the fisherman his sail unfurled,
The goat-herd drove his kids to steep Ben Goil,
Before the hut the dame her spindle twirled,
Courting the sunbeam as she plied her toil;
For, wake where'er he may, Man wakes to care and toil."

Glen Chalmadale, opening behind Loch Ranza, is the picturesque road to Glen Sannox and Corrie.

Five hundred years ago the square dark thick-walled tower that occupies the peninsula stretching across the bay was the hunting seat of Scottish kings, who must have had a wonderful selection of them. Further south, below the headland of Drumadoon, are the King's Caves which sheltered Bruce, and at the extreme southern point of the island is Kildonan, once "eyrie of the island lords," now a signalling station for passing ships, for whom at night, five furlongs off, the lighthouse burns on Pladda.

Keats, referring to Arran, wrote of it as one of the Hebrides, an allusion which must surprise all but those who remember that it was, like Rathlin, South Kintyre, and the Isle of Man, comprised in the old Hebridean archipelago, though to-day, of course, the term is more restricted. If Arran is no longer of the Hebrides, it curiously perpetuates in many ways the Hebridean character. Less than ten miles from the lowland shire of Ayr, standing in the fairway of one of the great portals of Empire, within two hours travel of Glasgow, whose citizens make as much of a playground of it as the laird will allow or they can afford, and beat upon by a myriad immediate lowland influences, it yet remains distinctively of the old Gaelic world. Geologists have found in Arran an epitome of the British Isles, and botanists have not exhausted its interest. The ethnologist and the student of tongues have hardly yet discovered its significance as illustrating the persistency of racial types, and the mutations of Celtic dialect.

THE HOMEWARD BOUND, OFF AILSA CRAIG

That the people of the island should be Gaels, as the Brandanes of Bute and the folk of the Cowal shore have long ceased to be in anything but an hereditary sense, is perhaps as much due to the policy of its landlords as to any inherent stability in the race. If Arran itself and the great city where it shops had their way, the quiet island shores to-day would be as populous as those of the mainland. It has been a grudge against the Hamiltons that they should scrupulously preserve this insular estate of theirs from the villa and the crowd, but the policy is not without its justification in the eyes of all who in nature love the primitive and wild, and prize an occasional hour of solitude.

Farming and fishing remain as of old the chief pursuits of Arran, though the cottagers have added to their incomes—and perhaps also to their sophistication—by intercourse with the summer lodger. Gaelic persists in three different dialects—that of the north island, the south end, and Shiskin, and the genuine old Gaelic spoken everywhere is very old and valuable, though recent mixed formations are unhappily increasing. Folk-tale and "ceilidh"—the old gossip gatherings of the crofting communities—are things of the past, but the people still preserve their Gaelic proverbs, and the Free Kirk has not wholly rid them of old, interesting, and inoffensive superstitions.

If Keats found Burns's apathy to Arran a thing to wonder at, he had learned himself—from Scott, perhaps—the emotional value of the sublime in Scottish scenery, and Arran duly impressed him. But it was to a tinier isle of the Firth he paid his poetic compliments. On his pedestrian tour to Scotland in 1818, walking one day from Girvan to Ballantrae, he saw on a sudden on his left, far out at sea, the rock which generations of Scots mariners have known as "Paddy's Milestone." "Really, I was a little alarmed," he wrote to his brother afterwards—why, we cannot guess, for Ailsa Craig is a lumpish, harmless-looking monster —and in the inn that evening he wrote the sonnet:

"Hearken, thou craggy ocean pyramid!
Give answer from thy voice—the sea-fowls' screams!
When were thy shoulders mantled in huge streams?
When, from the sun, was thy broad forehead hid?
How long is't since the mighty power bid
Thee heave to airy sleep from fathom dreams—
Sleep in the lap of thunder or sunbeams—
Or when grey clouds are thy cold coverlid!
Thou answer'st not; for thou art dead asleep;
Thy life is but two dead eternities—
The last in air, the former in the deep;
First with the whales, last with the eagle-skies—
Drown'd wast thou till an earthquake made thee steep,
Another cannot wake thy giant size."

But recently the West of Scotland roused with indignation to the possibility of the second "dead eternity" of the Craig being checked incontinent by soulless quarrymasters, but though its columnar trap has for years been used for the making of curling-stones, and more extensive quarrying is in prospect, the rock, which, twelve miles south of Pladda and ten from Girvan, lifts its forehead 1114 feet above the mean level of the tides, is unlikely to be much affected in its aspect from the sea, or rendered the less secure a sanctuary for the birds that people its shelves and crevices. A single incident—grotesque to incredibility—gives it a place on the page of history. In the closing years of the sixteenth century a crack-brained Barclay, Laird of Ladyland in Ayrshire, apostate from the reformed faith, connived with Roman Catholics in Spain, France, England, and at home to take possession of Ailsa Craig and "set upp and manteyne ane publique masse in this island, whilk should be patent to all distressed papists" and likewise provide "ane place of releife and refreshment to the Spanyart, or rather a porte to them, at ther arryvall in Ireland." A Paisley parson named Knox, whose foible was the hunting down of Jesuitry, "seminarie preistis and suspect trafficqaris with the King of Spayne," secretly stationed himself and nineteen others on the rock and beat off Barclay's party, drowning the laird of Ladyland himself. So Ailsa Craig lost the chance of becoming a fortress republic for the cure of souls, but its beacon winks at night and its sirens blare for the safety of all human voyagers.

THE END.

INDEX

Index

Index

Lightning Source UK Ltd.
Milton Keynes UK
UKHW021321010222
398036UK00009B/271

9 781845 300845